TO BE FAIR

Contemplations of an Inconvenient Missionary

C Stephens

To Be Fair

© 2023 C Stephens

ISBN-13: 978-1-998970-70-4 (Paperback)
ISBN-13: 978-1-998970-72-8 (PDF)
ISBN-13: 978-1-998970-71-1 (Ebook)

Typeset in 10/12 Sabon by Mbokodo Publishers
Printed by Mbokodo Publishers 1 2 3 4 5 1 2

Every effort has been made to obtain copyright permission for material used in this book. Please contact the Author with any queries in this regard.

Dedication

This book is dedicated
to the memories of
Malintzin, Pocahontas and Krotoa

TO BE FAIR

Contemplations of an Inconvenient Missionary

Contents

Preamble

Rejoice and be exceedingly glad

I am not a saint; I am a Christian missionary. I am human, and as such, imperfect. But I have always been inspired by hearing tales of the pioneers of my vocation.

I disagree with the prevailing misconceptions about missionaries – in the 21st century. I read this bias as part of a larger narrative that is revisionist – with the intent to weaken or even sink the church. Globalism wants to get rid of religion in general, and Christianity in particular.

Especially when churches are being burned down and Christians locked up for speaking out prophetically. Free speech is being labeled hate speech. This has gone beyond the issue of civil liberties, the church is being singled out. God knows the residential schools debacle has been bad enough. But piling unproven innuendo onto that is incendiary. My logic is simple – why would so many people whose careers spring from high levels of altruism and religious zeal commit psychopathic crimes right on the mission field? This makes about as much sense to me as defunding the police, as the panacea to restoring the rule of law. To be fair, I want to see a full not just a partial narrative.

A caveat is necessary here. In any and every vocation, there are individuals who are corrupt. "Corruption" is a huge problem in South Africa, and people generalize "the ANC is totally corrupt". Well, it clearly has many corrupt individuals. And malpractice is prevalent. But can it legitimately be said *the whole ANC* – a broad church alliance with heroes like John Dube, Albert Luthuli, Oliver Tambo and Nelson Mandela – is corrupt? This is why the narrative disturbs me that all priests, nuns, teachers and support staff were universally abusive. We know crimes were committed by individuals, even Jean Vanier. Does that de-legitimize the whole of L'Arche? In other words, are we throwing out the clean baby with the dirty bathwater?

Will Canada scrap hockey as its national sport because of the recklessness of some individual hockey players? Are they all like that, each and every one? To what extent is a game or a vocation brought into disrepute by the reprobate behavior of individuals?

So I have decided to create a collage – a mosaic. This contains only snapshots of women and men across the ages who have sacrificed selflessly to bring good news to the poor. Science-based health care and education for all.

At one stage I was so vexed by the revisionism about missionaries, I wrote a poem and submitted it for the Montreal Poetry Prize – in 2022. It did not win any award, except possibly the booby prize. Because in 2021 - 2022, "woke" ideology was blooming. Thank God there is now push-back.

One exposé that emerged around this time was "the Chilling Effect" – identified by human rights observatories in Europe and South Africa. Their research concluded the attack on Christianity is in fact discrimination. It violates the rights of people of faith. It actually tries to side-line or silence them.

This was done by declaring politically incorrect "witnessing", and worse yet, praying in public. Reports on this academic research were released, and within months there was a turn-over (that's a rugby term for you hockey fans out there!). The unrelated over-turning of *Roe v. Wade* came on the heels of the announcement of these research findings. This really set humanists and relativists on the back foot. For the church had worked and prayed feverishly against abortion, and suddenly the tides have begun to turn...

Let's be honest, in the 21st century, we are groping our way through various social issues which are having a polarizing effect on society. In the abortion debate you have pro-life versus pro-choice. Environmental issues still lack consensus. Even the Covid crisis has given rise to push-back over civil liberties and government overreach. There is a blazing conflict of ideas – like many other debates which have been so common in the history of Christianity. Biblical views engage with prevailing views of an era or culture somewhere. Infanticide in the Roman Empire (and much later in Tahiti when pioneer missionaries arrived there). Suttee in India. Foot-binding in China. These were widely practiced in those settings, but Christianity took exception. Simply because it didn't line up with their Bible. But suddenly in the 21st century, the tables have turned. What Christians believe has been challenged by secular and relativist narratives. And the debates have become extremely passionate and shrill. To the point that human rights observatories concluded anti-church sentiment has become discriminatory. So it is I wrote the poem I now use to set the tone of this book.

Fasten your seat-belts!

Backsliding Going Forward

We are the explorers, *we blaze the trails*

We befriend the inhabitants, we ask their guides for strategic intel

We give their women our babies

We are filled with wonder and awe

At what we see in our electron microscopes, dressed in our white labcoats

We research new widgets and technological innovation

We are the pioneers, *we clean out the underbrush*

We cut down the virgin forests, we exploit and export natural resources

We displace the indigenous folk, like Sapiens displaced Neanderthal

We immigrate through porous borders, we occupy the land

We frak the environment

With seismic exploration of the sea-bed

We are the missionaries, *we engage the native people*

We learn their language and esteem their culture

We try to practice what we preach about Justice

We live simply, so others can simply live

We beat their drums to call them to worship

We always try to look out for their best interests

10

We are the settlers. *We plant and harvest abundantly, in cleared fields*

We trade our pork bellies on the futures markets

We sell our farms so urban sprawl can swallow prime farm land

Changing the skyline forever, driving up prices in the housing bubbles

So our grandchildren can become urban serfs

While agriculture reverts to corporations

Who are the progenitors, who tear down statues?

They march, they loot, they burn, they convoy, they blockade

They re-write history

#ExplorersMustFall,#PioneersMustFall, #MissionariesMustFall

They believe Democracy should be run by minority lobbies

They swap the rule of law for government overreach

Ancestral worship for scientific revolution

Assimilation for alienation, tradition for trending

The wisdom of elders for the wit of youth

The rock of ages for invisible algorithms

Henry George for Greta Thunberg

Populist oligarchs and business tycoons for freely and fairly elected comedians

Their prophets say "Stay young, stay foolish" and "I was so much older then, I'm younger than that now"

What hominin are they? Denisovan? We don't know them.

But they are a legend in their own mind.

Since when do young fry generate folklore for a generation that knows better?

Then for Christmas 2022, I was given a book called <u>The Inconvenient Indian</u> as a gift. It was first published a decade earlier in 2012, but it has an afterword dated 2017. I love Thomas King's affable writing style and his broad scoping. I don't disagree the indigenous people of North America have been treated very shabbily by foreign invaders, whether colonial or after the intruders set up independent states.

The problem is my own personal experience, and my readings about the pioneers of my vocation, do not line up with the narrative that missionaries were there to minister to the white settlers alone and cooperated with secular powers to implement their racist agendas. Anyone who has seen the motion picture <u>The Mission</u> can make the simple distinction between the business interests of the big companies that were granted concessions as the colonial model of economic development; the powerful control-freaks of the colonial military forces (British, French, Dutch, Spanish, Portuguese, etc.); and the spiritual and moral motives of missionaries.

One of my sourcebooks is <u>On the Missionary Trail</u> by Tom Hiney. I owe him a debt of gratitude for unpacking so much from the annals of the London Missionary Society, on the occasion of its bi-centenary. Here is how he sums it up on page 329: "It is hard to see how men like Johannes Van der Kemp, who married the widow of a Madagascan slave and had assassination attempts made on him by white settlers, could in any way be seen as a stooge of imperialism."

I second the emotion. It is a narrative that just does not work for me. Of course missionaries used the ships and trains of business and commerce to reach the unreached. They used facilities like banking and colonial border posts just like anyone else. Just because we use a national airline or change money into a national currency does not mean we support all that government's policies. That is naïve. Story after story in the archives of missionaries relates how injustice was confronted, and how frequently colonial regimes were at odds with missionaries.

For example, the above cited Johannes Van der Kemp served as a kind of "observatory" – sending his accounts of injustices and mistreatment of the Khoi and the San people to an MP in British Parliament whose name was William Wilberforce. The evangelical press in England was full of his exposés and this embarrassed the British government. They were a cause-and-effect catalyst to policy change. In other words, my calculations are very different from the revisionist narrative. I believe it starts with an axe to grind and puts a very nasty spin on history. As much as anything, this is done by ignoring or omitting historical facts that do not support the revisionist narrative.

In a world of propaganda, Truth is a conspiracy theory.

So I decided just to collect some typical profiles and present them in a way that is not in sync with the revisionist narrative. In doing so, I rejoice in my vocation and I am glad for its forefathers and foremothers.

"Blessed are ye when men shall revile you, and persecute you, and shall say all manner of evil against you falsely, for my sake. Rejoice, and be exceedingly glad" Mathew 5:11,12.

Methodology

The whole truth and nothing but

This book is a mosaic, a patchwork quilt. I am more a collector of history than a true researcher. But I do have experience in social research. I can collate data and squeeze meaning from it – information.

One thing I learned is when incoming samples of data no longer change the findings and conclusions your preliminary interpretation has led to, then there is no point in spending more time and money on collecting more data. You reach a saturation point. A critical mass. This is not like counting votes – which involves counting every last ballot - until each and every voter is heard from. Social research is more impressionistic. And one good rule is not to go into it any deeper than the resources of time and money allow. The word "sampling" says it all. Get enough to be accurate, but not so much that it overwhelms you with collating work. That is what I decided to do – collect a wide sampling of missionary profiles. From history, not from fiction. And to present them in such a way the reader can see what is evident – missionaries are not sinister or duplicitous, on the whole. Their ethical standards tend to be high – what we once called "noble". But this vocation has often been at odds with other interests, so I admit its reputation is controversial.

At the end of the Gospel of John there are two verses which seem to be contradictory, but they capture this methodology...

The last two verses of chapter 20: "Jesus performed many other signs in the presence of his disciples, which are not recorded in this book. But these are written that you may believe..."

Then the last two verses of John's Gospel: "This is the disciple who testifies to these things and who wrote them down. We know that his testimony is true. Jesus did many other things as well. If every one of them were written down, I suppose that even the whole world would not have room for the books that would be written."

Obviously, St John had never heard of "the Cloud". Which must contain a good proportion of all the books ever written – and it is still growing! But I think the point he was making is that the Jesus movement was fanning out, all over the known world, taking the Good News far and wide – with signs and wonders everywhere. This Jesus movement starts in first gear in the Book of Acts when the arrival of the promised Holy Spirit is awaited. John and Peter heal a blind man on their way to the temple. James Boanerges is conspicuous by his absence. It is possible he was already on a missionary journey by then.

Then Pentecost gets the Jesus movement into second gear. Because the three thousand people baptized by fire on that day are from all over the Mediterranean. They take the Good News back to their places of origin. Sometimes missionaries are not "sent" but they are converted while abroad, and then return home carrying the Gospel with them. On this note, history repeats itself time and again. It even becomes a strategy for reaching "closed" countries.

Third gear is triggered by the Great Commission. Out of which comes the "apostolic comity agreement". Each of those who Jesus trained goes off in a different direction. This was not just random. It is how it was rolled out, very intentionally and collaboratively. Severally, not jointly.

The Book of Acts is a very early record of the A-team's travels under this apostolic comity agreement. (Of course, the A in "A-team" is for apostle.) Written by Dr. Luke, who also wrote one of the four Gospels, we get compelling accounts of these early missionary journeys.

Fourth gear is engaged when the churches planted by the wave of apostles mature and begin to send out their own missionaries. There are amazing samples of this happening down through the ages. It comes in waves. This gives rise to the term "the three-self church" – self-sustaining, self-governing and self-propagating. The third self is where missionaries are deployed.

Then comes fifth gear – the Modern Missionary Movement. This wave still has a lot of momentum, which started a little before Napoleon was defeated by the British. By this time, the whole world was discovered but not wholly colonized. In the following decades, Britannia ruled the waves, and the sun never set on the British Empire. First European and British, then later American missionaries spread out under the *Pax Britannica*, as the A-Team had spread out under the *Pax Romana*. Only glimpses of what they did are contained in the samples I have scoped and included in this book.

They are enough that you might question the inadequacy of the revisionist narrative, or even change your mind.

But I don't suppose all the books in the whole world could contain all the stories about all the missionaries who have served in this vocation.

Sound familiar? It is, because the church is the mystical body of Christ and missionaries are his ambassadors. Just as God *sent* his son and then received him back into the Holy Trinity, the church sends and receives missionaries. From all nations. To all nations. This is a blessed vocation, which is at times reviled, persecuted and sullied... for which we should only rejoice and be glad.

There are lots of jokes about lawyers. A lot of these jokes are not very nice, especially if you happen to be a lawyer yourself. People may re-tell these jokes, but hopefully not in the presence of lawyers? What can you do when prejudice rises like this, against your whole vocation? Maybe there is some truth to this comedy, because every vocation will have its imposters or charlatans. But when the law comes for you, there is no substitute for a good lawyer.

In the last chapter, I wrote: "In a world of propaganda, Truth is a conspiracy theory." This one-liner prompted an old friend of mine to explain to me:

"We live in an age when Truth can be possessed. Folks don't talk about "*the truth*" anymore. They talk about "*my truth*" or "*his truth*" or "*her truth*". Sometimes a tribe has a collective truth. That would be "*their truth*". This is not exactly relativism. If a person can "*self-identify*" as anything or anyone they choose, then it is easy to add a story. The story becomes "*his truth*" or "*her truth*" and people are expected not to question it. If they do, they are attacking the tribe, with which that person has self-identified. Of course, in the process, truth, in any absolute or even relative sense, ceases to exist.

I think we should pass a law – the use of the possessive with the word *"Truth"* is illegal. You cannot own truth. It belongs to us all. We might know it all, very likely we don't. But only the insufferably proud would claim what they don't know doesn't exist. This is relevant because the willingness of many to accept an incomplete story, and to excoriate anyone who does not, is a good example of a claim to *"possess truth"*. We are expected to accept what he says, because it is *"his truth"*, and woe be unto you if you do not. Of course, this idea of possessive truth, varying with the possessor, is irreconcilable with the Christian faith. We know *"the"* truth ... the way and the life. It is not different from one Christian to another, and in that sense, none of us *"own"* the truth."

I have included a heavy dose of perspectives and missionary lore from other continents, not just North America. I do this partly because I myself was born and raised in Africa, so I know it first-hand. Especially its missionary dimensions, as I was born of parents who were Canadian medical missionaries serving in the Belgian Congo. However, I see this as a kind of "control experiment". For the missionary outreach which originated in Europe did not function one way in South Africa and another way in Canada. Particularly before the proliferation of mission organizations began. Early on, there were rather bigger mission entities such as the

London Missionary Society. I suppose they were trying to be the church equivalent of the large business concessions like the Hudson's Bay Company or the Dutch East India Company? So the LMS deployed missionaries in Africa, Latin America, Asia and the South Seas. This in itself was useful because they could learn what works best by comparing activities and results from different "mission fields". For example, twenty years after sending out its first missionaries, two evaluators were dispatched from London. An evaluation team. There were no planes in those days so their remit took two years. A great deal was recorded and learned from this exercise. Two centuries later, this serves as an excellent source of missionary lore.

Similarly, I think it is fair to say missionaries who set out in the same era to North or South America were cut from the same cloth, so to speak. I see more variations occurring as a result of macro-changes over time (e.g. Protestant Reformation, Counter-Reformation, Industrial Revolution, and the Enlightenment) than I do from one continent to another. So, it is useful in my view to check what the "gold standard" was for any given era, when missionaries on one continent suddenly suffer huge reputation loss.

And I am humble enough to say we got it wrong at times. The conflict between Catholics and Protestants was carried to some colonies – where people went to escape it! The tacit endorsement of colonial policy by our guilty silence. We sometimes cowered when we should have spoken up. And the relatively recent residential schools debacle, where Christian missionaries became instruments of government policy instead of calling out this nightmare. And apartheid, which was condoned by some churches until other churches sounded the alarm that is was heretical.

Still through all this, sincere missionary motives survived, giving us the humility to fail forward. The baseline of outreach remained in place – learn the vernacular, translate the Bible, teach literacy so the constituency can read the Bible, then provide additional services – usually in learning and healing.

This has rolled out in different ways, in different places and at different times. But the common denominator has always been there. So we will keep our eye on the success formula, which was abandoned at times to the detriment of our vocation. We want to highlight successes that go unmentioned in the revisionist narrative, because they don't fit. If this was lying by omission, we claim the right of reply. If it was just an honest effort at debate, we engage by presenting an overview of our evidence.

This book is not about the indigenous peoples of North America. My focus is much narrower. My focus is prejudice – not against these First Nations but against missionaries. As illuminated in the pages of <u>The Inconvenient Indian</u>. Which incidentally is a book worth reading. I especially like chapter 7 – perhaps because I could now remember the events (post-1985). I was living in Winnipeg when Elijah Harper voted down the Meech Lake accord. Holding a feather, if I remember correctly?

But in the whole 28 pages of chapter 7 - packed with facts that flow from a well-informed author – there was only one jab at Christianity, the church or missionaries. After six chapters of holding, hooking, roughing and charging, Thomas King plays some serious ice hockey in chapter 7, there's just that one pointless body-check. Otherwise, he really knows his stuff. Except for his Bible. He says there are no verses that explicitly teach us how to confront hate. I contest that. Check out these seventeen verses for a start:

- Leviticus 19: 17,18

- Proverbs 10:12

- Proverbs 15:1

- Ecclesiastes 3: 7,8

- Matthew 5:44

- Luke 6: 22,23

- Luke 6: 27,28

- Romans 12:14

- Ephesians 4:31

- 1 Peter 2:19,21

- 1 John 3:15

I got to wondering why he inserted the two paragraphs on pages 196 and 197 at all? Two paragraphs in 28 pages of text (not counting the full-page plates). He admits he doesn't understand how "turning the other cheek" helps. That is sadly apparent. In a long 28-page review of relatively recent (post-1985) policy, he can't resist taking another swipe at the Bible.

An author who is writing to expose prejudice against his people should be above prejudice against other people.

I agree with Thomas King on many issues. But I don't agree with the way he lumps Christianity with colonialism or with detrimental government policies. However, I do respect his other views. In the following pages, I treat him as a spokesperson for revisionism about missionaries in general. I don't think this aspect adds even a tad of value to his book, if anything it alienates a lot of readers. Like me. But I persisted because the book is comprehensive in scope and is passionately written. I am a missionary, and I weep about injustice. But it is hard to weep when someone keeps slapping you in the face!

A distinction must be made between prejudice and lying-by-omission. Having a preconceived opinion is bad. Deliberately misleading is worse. In this regard, spokesman Thomas King is the prosecutor, I am advocating for the defense, and the reader is the judge. Sometimes prosecutors omit things because they don't know about them until the defense introduces evidence. But some prosecutors just leave it to the defense to bring up certain points, even when they know about them. That is tactical deceit. It is why the defense needs to be heard. Just how much of his silence is because he didn't know, or whether he isn't saying because it doesn't fit his narrative, is unknown to me. All I know is there are glaring gaps. I owe him a vote of thanks for serving as my spokesperson for revisionism, in this regard. It's easier to conduct a debate with two speakers. By detecting the gaps, I can fill them in. Which is what I am trying to do.

This fits my primary purpose in writing – to round up the stories of a controversial vocation.

1. THE A-TEAM

A is for Apostle

As I have already written two books about this amazing team of women and men, I will only outline the relevance of this iconic movement to the controversial missionary vocation.

Papyrus Pen Pals

The apostolic comity agreement was the game-plan of the A-Team:

- Thomas went east to India (the Mar-Toma church still exists today)

- Matthew went south to Nubia – in those days the term "Ethiopia" referred to what we know today as Africa. What we call Ethiopia today was then called Abyssinia. The eunuch who Philip baptizes in the Book of Acts was from Nubia. At that time, the capital of Nubia was Moroe

- Simon of Cana headed west, through the Gates of Hercules (i.e. Gibraltar) and around the Iberian Peninsula to England

- Andrew went north through the Dardanelles and across the Hospitable Sea (i.e. the Black Sea) to Crimea and inland to Scythia (what we now call the Ukraine and Russia)

The name Hospitable Sea was a euphemism, because it used to be called the Inhospitable Sea. Seven of the twelve disciples were Galilean fisherman, so they were right at home on sea voyages. But the A-Team was equally divided between women and men, as I go to great lengths to document in my earlier writing.

Bones of Contention

Then I wrote a second book – not about their lives and times, but about how they died. And thereafter, where they were buried. And re-buried. For their relics were and are revered, so as macro-factors changed, so did their resting places. For example, John Mark was from North Africa. He became the first bishop of Egypt, based in the relatively new city of Alexandria. That is where he was buried. But centuries later, Islam spread like a veld fire across North

27

Africa. So Christians from Venice decided to move his relics where they could keep them safe. Thus we have St Mark's square in Venice today. Across the sea, far from his place of birth and original burial on the south shore of the Mediterranean.

Most of the A-team died horrific deaths in an age of persecution. The church was still banned. It was underground, both metaphorically speaking and in real catacombs. It was only un-banned and nationalized some three hundred years later by the emperor Constantine. He built the great basilica in Constantinople (i.e. now Istanbul) to gather into one place the relics of the A-Team. Where he could be buried with them, of course.

However, in due course Islam overran this great Roman city, so relics were moved to safety in Italy and Europe. What was once the epicentre of Roman Christianity – that great basilica – became a mosque. Times change. The church is affected by various secular, cultural and military forces. Its fortunes change.

As I see it, the A-Team set a high bar for future missionary work. It did not just stick to the Roman world, although surely Roman roads and its rule of law created the conditions for missionary outreach. For three centuries, Christianity experienced waves of persecution. Monotheism was a great threat to Rome's polytheism. Christians challenged some Roman practices – like infanticide. The Gospel of Love was clearly a challenge to the Roman system of Justice. Although the notion of Grace could not have arrived at a better time – when military might enforced Roman laws. Grace was indeed a contrast and it prevailed, in the long run.

My two books are based on some reading and research I did for my doctorate (D.Litt). The period from the end of the Book of Acts to the death of the last of the Twelve around 100 AD is very far in the past. But it is very well documented and not only in the New Testament. Some Christians admit the "extra-biblical" sources, others prefer the *sola scriptura* approach. While such controversies raged inside church circles, Christian outreach still had a subversive effect on the *status quo*.

Constantine, of course, organized a number of church councils to try to harmonize and standardize the faith. Unfortunately, this caused many extra-biblical sources to be destroyed, as a *canon* of the Scriptures emerged. Brought to you by "orthodoxy". That was a poor excuse for burning good books. There was no such thing at the time of the A-Team. They only had one another to filter out the apocryphal stories. Their leader was gone – not only

29

executed and buried, but victorious over death and ascended into heaven.

Were they too critical of the *status quos* they encountered on their missionary journeys? Or were they just too zealous to preach monotheism to polytheists and love and grace to law-abiding Romans? Why did they all have such a similar end-of-life martyrdom, across such a wide geography, even outside the Roman world in the Parthian sphere, and beyond? And why did this not cause the collapse of their mission?

An African called Tertullian replied famously to these questions: "The blood of martyrs is seed" (*Apologeticum*, 50). Incidentally, Tertullian was the first Christian writer to use the term "trinity". This term does not appear in the scriptures. It was his way of explaining the way he read the Word. Please note I am not talking theology here, I am talking "missiology". How missionaries work, not what the Word says or means. I recognize this term Trinity has become highly controversial and contentious – first between the Roman church and the Eastern Orthodox church, and later between Christians and Muslims.

Mission work must interpret the Good News to its constituents. From the four Gospel-writers on, to those missionaries who travelled far and wide, to those of them who wrote pastoral letters (i.e. epistles), this interpretation or "unpacking" is at the forefront. Each Gospel was written for a different audience, and thus there are some apparent discrepancies. But on the whole, they harmonize. Each epistle was also to a specific church or cultural group. For example, the letter to the Ephesians was for believers in the city of Ephesus specifically, but is still classic teaching, twenty centuries on. And the letter to the Hebrews was written specifically to Jews, knowing that Gentiles might not have the same deep background in Hebrew literature and history which Jews have.

I think the gold standard set by the A-team has one aspect in particular that is mission-critical to all future outreach. That is its bi-cultural nature. St Paul is a great example, as he was both a devout Jew and a Roman citizen. Remember John the Baptist and Jesus were not Roman citizens, so they were relatively easy to take out by unscrupulous local leaders. On the other hand, Paul was basically "bullet-proof" because of his Roman citizenship. Until he got to Rome, that is.

When James the brother of Jesus learned that Paul was a Roman citizen and thus more protected than his brother/master had been, some tension emerged. I am not sure whether that was just surprise, because Paul had always shined up his Jewish credentials whenever he was in Jerusalem? Or was there a bit of resentment creeping in, that

Paul was entitled to appeal his case to the Caesar, a right that Jesus had not enjoyed? (Pontius Pilate basically had the last word with Jesus, which he devolved to the Jewish leaders, by washing his hands.) Whereas Paul's trial would be before Procurator Antonius Felix in Caesarea Maritima, the Roman capital of Palestine at the time. (Jerusalem was only the Jewish capital.) Paul had the right of appeal to the Caesar.

Or as the *de facto* bishop at that time, was it sinking into James' thinking Paul could be on his way to stand before the Caesar and preach the Gospel to him? For which there would be repercussions.

I remember when Paul visited Athens, he went to Mars Hill where all the various Greek temples were. He went to the temple of the unknown god. I guess for the Greeks, it was sort of an insurance policy in their framework of polytheism, in case they had missed one? This shows he wanted to engage local culture on its own terms. This is the essence of missionary work. You have to learn the local language, appreciate local customs and culinary treats, and to present the Good News in that context.

When you step out of your own culture and into another, there are risks. Your flawed accent might give away the fact that you are a foreigner. Beware xenophobia. Worst of all, you might discover facets of that culture which are incompatible with Christian beliefs and values. The example of infanticide comes to mind in the Roman world. It was so common in Rome that women going down to the Tiber River to wash their laundry complained about the dead babies floating by. If you didn't want a child, just throw them into the Tiber. Christianity confronted this social/moral evil and ultimately defeated it. While at the same time converting Rome from polytheism to monotheism.

Mission work gets complicated, but we have some great role-models who set the gold standard. Thomas King gives an example of the inhospitable reception that Christianity can still get, on page 75. "An outfit called "Hellish Family" will sell you a T-shirt that has a crucifixion scene on the back with "Seven Generations" at the top and "You Are Not My Christ" at the bottom for $12.95."

The *Seventh Generation* takes its name from the Great Law of the Haudenosaunee, the founding document of the Iroquois Confederacy. The Oneida, Mohawk, Seneca, Onondaga and Cayuga (and later in the 1700s, the Tuscarora) had been in conflict against each other. It was a period of great instability, which continued until the arrival of the Peacemaker (Hiawatha), who brought the Great Law of Peace, uniting the warring nations (circa 1142 AD) and forming the Haudenosaunee (Iroquois) Confederacy. It was a model of federalism which influenced the emergence of the constitution of the USA.

The seventh generation principle is wise and enduring. Decisions taken today should lead to a sustainable peace for the next seven generations.

The best way to reach the unreached in this context would have been to preach to the Iroquois Confederacy the Good News about the Prince of Peace. In the Sermon on the Mount, Jesus teaches non-violence, love and grace. That is the Way Forward, for seventy-seven generations...

Try to find one another. Seek sustainable peace. The Bible calls it *shalom*.

Hats off to Benjamin Franklin, who printed the following 1744 speech by Onondaga leader Canassatego for the 1754 Albany Congress, at which Franklin presented his Plan of Union:

"We heartily recommend Union and a good Agreement between you our Brethren. Never disagree, but preserve a strict Friendship for one another, and thereby you, as well as we, will become the stronger. Our wise Forefathers established Union and Amity between the Five Nations; this has made us formidable; this has given us great Weight and Authority with our neighboring Nations. We are a powerful Confederacy; and, by your observing the same Methods our wise Forefathers have taken, you will acquire fresh Strength and Power; therefore whatever befalls you, never fall out one with another."

2. THE DESERT FATHERS

From Hebrew and Greek to Coptic

No scan of missionary motives and history would be complete without coverage of the self-denialists.

The hermits of Egypt laid the foundation for the later monastic orders. They were ascetics, in the tradition of John the Baptist. And as in the Jesus movement from its origins, women were very active – there were desert nuns as well as monks. These were the mamas and the papas (ammas and abbas) of Christianity:

- Paul of Thebes

- St Anthony the Great

- Arsenius the Great

- Poemen

- Macarius of Egypt

- Moses the Black

- Syncletica of Alexandria

- Pachomius

- Abba Or

- Shenoute of Atripe

- John Crysostom

- Evagrius Ponticus

- Hilarion

- St Amun

- John Cassian

These role-models had a huge influence on church history, starting in their own day and age. One controversial church leader called Athanasius of Alexandria, wrote "the desert had become a city".

They gave their lives entirely over to prayer, charity and counseling. The difference between these ammas and abbas and the original A-Team is the world was gradually Christianizing. Not only in the West, but in the East also. Including Africa and the Nile valley south (up-river) to Nubia too. So while there were still pockets of hostility, it was not a panorama of persecution anymore. So they were able to operate in a higher gear than the low gear of the apostles.

As my central focus in this book is psychological and spiritual, we can only point out a discrepancy. How can you reconcile the erstwhile motives of such fervent missionaries as the abbas and ammas with a narrative alleging this same vocation later degenerated into mass murder of children buried in unmarked graves on the school ground? This prospect is very disturbing to those of us who believe in the communion of saints and in the integrity of our vocation. It's incompatible.

Christianity seemed to adapt well to various cultures. The demand that Christians become Jewish (i.e. circumcised) had been dropped early (at the first Council of Jerusalem in the Book of Acts chapter 15). There was no need to take on a dominant culture or language. Christianity spread *because* it was culturally relativist. So in later centuries you had not only the Christianization of Africa, but also the Africanization of Christianity. This is good missiology.

Reading The Inconvenient Indian made me wonder a lot about missiology. When Thomas King writes about the Lone Ranger (white) and Tonto (red), he says on page 50: "Sure, the Ranger called the shots, but Tonto rode as well, fought as well, shot as well as the Ranger, and he had skills that the Ranger did not."

"Tonto's character simply affirmed North American history and celebrated the forward thrust of progress. It was proof positive that as Indians were gently pressed through the sieve of civilization, they would come out looking and sounding like Tonto."

As I think of the Roman Empire, I know emperors came from various cultural and geographical origins throughout the Empire - including Africa. They did not all come from Rome, or even Italy. I do not see cultural hegemony in this, although they all did need to learn Latin and so on. If the Roman Empire had spread to North America, could an indigenous person not have become emperor? Segregation has had a way of excluding indigenous people from governance. Whereas a fundamental democratic principle is that those who are affected by a decision should have a voice in the decision-making process.

Thomas King writes on page 70: "In order to maintain the cult and sanctity of the Dead Indian, North America has decided that Live Indians living today cannot be genuine Indians. This sentiment is a curious reworking of one of the cornerstones of Christianity, the idea of innocence and original sin. Dead Indians are Garden of Eden-variety Indians. Pure, Noble, Innocent. Not a feather out of place. Live Indians are fallen Indians, modern, contemporary copies, not authentic Indians at all, Indians by biological association only."

Ouch! Well if the Desert Mothers and Fathers were among the cornerstones of Christianity, I would say it set the stage for cultural relativism, not for cultural hegemony. They were not Jews or Greeks, they were Coptics. Egypt let go of polytheism for monotheism. And Christianity embraced Coptic. In his epistle to the Romans chapter 5, St Paul unpacks this doctrine – that as Sin came into the world through one man (Adam) affecting everybody thereafter, so also Grace came into the world by one man (Jesus) – for all. Grace is for everybody. Jews and Gentiles. Women and men. Blacks and whites. And most certainly for the First Nations of America as well.

St Paul – a Jew from Tarsus (in Turkey) – was a Roman citizen. And he was no stranger to the desert. For after his conversion on the road to Damascus, he launched his ministry into "Arabia" (today's Jordan). He gained experience there which helped him – among others – to shape Christianity into a new world religion *for all*. Not just into another sect of Judaism. This egalitarianism is in the DNA of the Christian church. The Gospel is inclusive.

Twenty centuries later, I grew up singing a simple chorus:

Jesus loves the little children

All the children of the world,

Red and yellow, black and white

All are precious in his sight

Jesus loves the little children of the world.

So how did a vocation with its roots in cultural relativism morph into something quite so ugly as the mass murder of children and even burying them anonymously? It just doesn't add up.

We tend to think of missionaries as being "sent". They go out to the mission frontier. We are less likely to appreciate that missionaries can also be "received". The desert mothers and fathers were not "sent missionaries" like Thomas going to India or Simon of Cana sailing to England. Missionaries must be received – somewhere, by someone. Including those of us serving in the here and now. Sometimes the reception is hostile, but not always. Armenia welcomed Christianity early on and became the first nation to call itself Christian. Egypt of course had a long history of polytheism, and a huge Jewish community embedded in Alexandria. As the centuries passed, it became tolerant of Christianity (especially after

Constantine's conversion). As did much of North Africa and the larger Mediterranean basin. So this created the conditions for ascetics who wanted to build character and offer compassionate care in their respective locations.

If we don't like the idea of receiving missionaries into our midst, and hearing them out, and would prefer they be "sent" (i.e. that they go away) - then we might be inclining towards cultural hegemony. The perennial two-way street of Christian missions is captured by the lyrics of the Servant Song:

Won't you let me be your servant?

Let me be as Christ to you

Pray that I might have the grace

To let you be my servant, too.

Attracting people into the Jesus movement is sometimes called "presence evangelism". As opposed to "proclamation evangelism" which involves actively reaching out to the unreached. In our day and age, radio stations beam the Gospel message into countries where the reception to missionaries would be hostile. In other places, Christian agencies deliver food aid and pro-poor development projects.

The sectors of learning and healing have largely become government functions, although these were once emphasized by Christian missions. This vocation is dynamic, adapting to the times.

The Desert Mothers and Fathers used the technology and resources of their era – and their own language - to consolidate the gains Christian outreach had made by then. There is a psychological and spiritual disconnect between their selfless service and the narrative of mistreatment of the indigenous people of Canada and the USA by missionaries. The two do not belong in the same vocation. They are irreconcilable.

As I read Thomas King's book, "Dead Indians" are those who are basically hospitable to Christianity, whereas "Live Indians" are inhospitable and reject it in favour of their own indigenous spirituality. Or of other faiths - monotheist or polytheist, secular or humanist. My understanding is that over half of the 2.6 million indigenous people in America now live off-reservation. Some of these may have assimilated to some degree. Others may just need employment. But those who put their roots down off-reservation may not all be so-called Dead Indians. I think rather, the phrase Dead Indian is a parody of assimilation in general, which has been the prevailing government policy, punctuated by periods of annihilation and/or co-habitation (my choice of words).

The role of missionaries is to sow seed. To evangelize a new tribe, anywhere, you have to be able to communicate. That's where language study begins. Which leads on to Bible translation, literacy training, and to broader learning in general. Consolidation (i.e. a broadening of services) comes in different forms after the church becomes established. Like offering counseling, vocational training, disaster relief, and advocacy for justice and peace (to mention only a few). In some cases, starting with Armenia, whole Christian nations emerge. So now children are born into Christianity, who do not need to be converted into it. They grow up in Christian homes, go to schools with Christian teachers and in turn, contribute to their society as a whole. They are recruited into the armies of those countries. Revisionists makes this sound like culture-bashing connivance. That is a *non sequiter*, as this has been happening for centuries, all around the world. For heaven's sake, Armenia is still a nation, with its own language and culture. And for its Christian beliefs and convictions, it has taken it on the cheek from the Turks and other Muslims. Yet it has remained faithful.

Missionary work is not coercion. It is the way the Gospel has spread far and wide. Christian outreach is the church's marketing function. Other religions and secular religions like humanism and Marxism do the same. It is the arena of ideas and world-views. It is open-season. Those who oppose it are the despots and diehards. Not the missionaries. It is ironic to me that wokeism wants to create conditions for the spread of humanism, relativism and even Marxism – while wanting to silence Christian outreach. This is a double-standard. But it is hard to speak of wokeism because it has so many strands.

Egyptian polytheism survived for not just centuries but millennia. One pharaoh called Akhenaten tried to switch over to monotheism, in the 14th century BC. By my calculation, this is when the children of Israel were occupying Goshen in the Nile Delta. I have often wondered if there is any connection? But the vested interests of organized religion were too strong, and for a long time, proactive revisionism erased him from the historical record. However Christian outreach really took hold of Egypt and Coptic Christianity became predominant for centuries. Until the rise of Islam, which reduced the Coptic church to about ten percent of Egypt's population today. What is gained by lamenting this? Egyptian identity still remains strong and distinct. Its history and culture are still vibrant. Coptic was supplanted by Arabic, which is spoken widely now, although several vernacular dialects still remain.

I highly recommend a visit to the Coptic Museum in Cairo. There is no shortage of things to see in that amazing city. But I enjoyed the Coptic Museum as much as any of Cairo's attractions.

Egypt has recently introduced its own "Camino" – a pilgrimage that follows the steps of the Holy Family as they fled from Herod's slaughter of the innocents. Until it was safe to return to Nazareth. One reason this new 21st century tourist attraction and spiritual experience is possible, is these sites were known to and recorded by the desert fathers and mothers.

One lesson learned from the missiology of this period is the foundational role of language study. This precedes Bible translation. Before you can have a Coptic Bible you need a Coptic dictionary.

There was not yet a definitive Latin Bible until this time – about 400 AD. Although there were partial translations into Old Latin, while the church was underground. On-going translation work was impeded by the dominance of Latin in the Middle Ages. But from Martin Luther's German translation in 1466 until a Serbian translation in 1936, Bible translation kept up momentum in Europe.

The Protestant Reformation emphasized vernacular translation of scripture and Protestant missionaries carried this remit far and wide. Then the Jesuits arose and added to this baseline of Christian outreach. In this respect, Latin was being slowly discarded. Both Protestants and some Catholics shared this strategy.

What a challenge in the "New World"! According to Wikipedia, there are over one thousand languages in the Americas. Some indigenous writing systems had started to develop – called "emblem glyphs". The Mayan writing system of Central America is the only one deciphered so far.

In the United States, 372,000 people reported speaking an indigenous language at home in the 2010 census. In Canada, 133,000 people reported speaking an Indigenous language at home in the 2011 census.

Indigenous people passed on their "stories" in art – beads, totem poles, masks, etc. This is not unique to indigenous culture. It prevails everywhere, including European art, which often tells a story. But, while the Chinese say, "*a picture is worth a thousand words*", don't believe it. A totem pole cannot tell the story of War and Peace in all its detail and nuance like Tolstoy. Written language uniquely enables expression in the broadest possible way.

Before the translation and literacy work can begin, it is necessary to create a written language. This is a gift to many indigenous peoples primarily from missionaries. It preserves a language and illuminates how people think. So it is salt and light to their culture. The benefits are being rediscovered today as indigenous peoples revive their languages. Written language is a vital part of human history. It enables the development of law with some certainty, the recording of history, art, and much, much more. It is increasingly common in Canada today to rename streets, schools and other institutions to delete colonial references and substitute indigenous names. That practice is possible only because written indigenous language exists thanks to the work of Christian missionaries.

The creating of a written language is among the greatest gifts given by missionaries. It has enabled so much more, and still does.

3. HOLY ORDERS

Brothers and mother-superiors, not just holy fathers

Inspired by Thomas King's insights into the fictional figure of Tonto, the Lone Ranger's companion, let me remind the reader of a similar, medieval side-kick who was large as life – Friar Tuck. He joined Robin Hood's band of merry men. He is an icon of the church's empathy with the poor. For Robin Hood's thing was to rob from the rich and give to the poor. Particularly when the rich were guilty of exploiting the poor.

There were plays and poems about Robin Hood, going back to the 15th century. The earliest fragment that still exists is from 1475. The oldest copy we have of the full poem "Robin Hood and the Curtal Friar" dates from the 17th century. We also have two royal writs from 1417 that refer to Robert Stafford, a Sussex chaplain who had assumed the alias of Frere Tuk. This "Friar Tuck" was still at large in 1429. These are the earliest surviving references to any character by that name. Whether Robert Stafford was the original or an impersonator, we will never know.

What exactly is a Curtal Friar? Probably "curtal" means "wearing a short frock". Like a mini-skirt. Monks and friars wore frocks or habits as part of the dress code of their vocation. This would have suited one of the bandits in Sherwood Forest. As a friar, he could not actively rob a bank, but he might agree to drive the get-away car? Is this an early version of liberation theology?

I am not a Roman Catholic, but I have read and studied about monasticism. Monasteries were the church infrastructure for monks and nuns. Whereas bishops and priests belonged in cathedrals or parish churches, in the tall diocesan structure. This was Rome's approach to church growth blending the ecclesiastical work of the padres with the community outreach work of the friars and madres.

This chapter quickly scans the thousand-year "medieval" era from 500 – 1500 AD. There was something of a split in the Roman church, but it was between East and West. The Protestant split didn't come until about 1500. So I will only highlight a few of the major monastic congregations that arose. It is fair to say health care, learning and orphan care *inter alia* centred on the monasteries during this period. Community outreach.

I went to seminary, but chose not to be ordained. Because I sensed my focus would be in the community, not in the church. Something like a "worker priest" or a "social worker". I wanted to be Charles Stephens, missionary. Friar Chuck.

The Holy Orders were a bit more free-wheeling in terms of their self-contained structure. As their remit was to be self-reliant, they were "cross-cutting" – that is, not a part of the diocesan hierarchy. But this does not mean they were un-disciplined. The Abbot in a monastery ruled the roost. Monasteries were not democratic at all, they were top-down. But they tended to be stand-alone, apart from the grid of parishes and dioceses. The rise of monasticism was concurrent to the crumbling of the Roman Empire, especially in western Europe. Commonly known as the Dark Ages. These two tracks of European history are inter-twined. An empire that used to be held together by military force was weakening and needed innovative ways to secure its legacy. Monasticism was one way to reinforce Rome's intellectual property, to keep educating future generations. Not to mention document storage.

What follows are merely impressionistic caricatures I offer from my limited exposure to monasticism. Nor is this list comprehensive, the Holy Orders mentioned are only samples. I only mention what seems to me to be relevant points. For I am trying to track down the deepest roots of the infamous residential schools that emerged at another time, in another place.

Augustinian nuns – St Augustine of Hippo (354 – 430 AD) started this community. His career path had taken him to Rome, but he chose to return to his home area in north Africa to make a start. Augustine was a Berber. Reclusive communities were already common in Egypt and the Levant, so St Augustine transplanted monasticism into the western empire, where it had to adapt to a different context. Augustine was born a century before St Patrick.

Benedictines – St Benedict of Nursia (480 – 548 AD) introduced the very strict Rule of St Benedict. Monks split their time between "ora" (prayer) and "labora" (work). This "Rule" was heavily influenced by John Cassia, so western monasticism did draw from the well of the Desert Fathers. Benedict got strong endorsements from Pope Gregory the Great and from Charlemagne. He had such huge influence, he is now the patron saint of Europe.

Benedictine monasteries would eventually be established far and wide, as opposed to church-planting. This could be in an area where the church was already present, to give depth to its overall ministry. Or new monasteries could be a way of reaching out, a kind of "preaching point" - to prepare mission fields for churches to follow suit.

Peregrini – As outlined in the next chapter, St Patrick evangelized Ireland. Then St Columba of Iona started a missions training centre to enable a new movement that re-evangelized Europe. The influence of these Celtic missionaries remained in Europe and merged with the overall structure of the Roman Catholic church. Its legacy continued to influence monasticism for several centuries after the Synod of Whitby in 664 AD.

Cistercians - Bernard of Clairvaux (1090–1153), principal founder of the Cistercian order, was trying to reform the Benedictine order. Just as in later times, the Capuchins would try to reform the Franciscan congregation. In both reforms, the trending was to recover austerity, to counter the growing wealth of the church. Bernard became the abbot of Clairvaux monastery in Bergundy in 1115 AD. He engaged widely in Europe and actively promoted the second Crusade.

Trappists – Armand Jean le Bouthillier de Rancé became the abbot of La Trappe abbey in Normandy in 1663. He led the Cistercians into deeper reforms, even more austerity. There are now seven Trappist abbeys in Canada and seventeen in the USA. However, the number of monks has been shrinking with rising secularization. A famous Trappist Monastery in

Oka, Quebec is now being converted into a Harry Potter theme park. This is symbolic of the rapid secularization of Quebec in particular.

Dominicans - Saint Dominic (1170–1221) founded his order in Spain. He was disturbed by the growing affluence of the church, including monasteries and abbeys. So his was the first mendicant (from Latin for begging) order, involving an oath of poverty for its monks and nuns.

On page 112 of his book, Thomas King writes a paragraph on the great debate that took place in Valladolid, Spain in 1550. One of the debaters was a Dominican bishop named Bortolome de las Casas. It is regrettable but typical that the propagandist omits telling his life story. As a youth, he was still in Spain when Columbus arrived back from his first voyage. He saw the seven "AmerIndians" whom Columbus brought back, along with other booty.

So he and his merchant father soon emigrated to Hispanola (today's Dominican Republic and Haiti) where they became landowners. He owned indigenous slaves. But in 1515 he gave them up - because of his Christian conviction that this was wrong. He later argued owning imported African slaves was wrong too.

He went on to join the Dominican order, becoming a friar and a social reformer. He was appointed as the first bishop in Chiapas in Mexico with a remit to become "protector of the Indians". He wrote extensive accounts of the atrocities against indigenous peoples of the West Indies. This is why he was invited to Valladolid, to debate a landowner named Juan de Sepulveda, who argued indigenous people were sub-human. They did not have souls, so they were natural slaves. The Dominican bishop won the debate with his contention that indigenous people do have souls, and slavery was wrong. How could this deep background be excluded? Silence can be conspicuous. Why fail to tell the truth about missionaries?

Franciscans - Saint Francis of Assisi (1181–1226) founded his order in Italy. He also disavowed the accumulation of personal wealth. Thus he is affectionately known as "the Poverello". He inspired an order of nuns that was founded by Saint Clare, commonly known as the "Poor Clares". In 1525, some Franciscans decided to return to the original rule of St Francis and changed their frocks or habits to have a hood. They are known as the Capuchins (for their hoods).

The church seemed to endure and prosper despite the decline of the western empire of Rome. The eastern empire was more Orthodox, and also included monasticism in honour of the Desert Fathers.

In all of their different ways, monasteries kept learning and healing alive throughout medieval times. Monasteries had libraries and actively copied manuscripts. Central and northern Europe were still largely unreached at the time of Augustine and Benedict. Missionaries like St Patrick and St Boniface set out to evangelize Ireland and Germany respectively. These were not nation-states at that time, as we know them today. They were vast areas populated by tribes speaking different dialects and languages. Not unlike North America when the missionaries arrived there. Monasteries were strategically sited among the tribes of Europe, not to subdue them but to preserve them.

This diversity is still evident in the nation-states of Europe. Switzerland has four official languages. Enclaves like Catalonia, Scotland and Basque country want to secede. Yugoslavia blew apart into a number of countries in the Balkans. Czechoslovakia ended up as two nations. What will happen to the Ukraine? Indigenous people cherish their language and culture. For the most part, the church has respected this diversity and reached out with due respect and care. It is true that Latin became a *lingua franca* for the church, but not to the exclusion of respect for local culture. There is a reason that aviation adopted one language for pilots. I need not even say which it is; the logic of having a *lingua franca* is self-evident. But this grip may have become too strong at times, in some places, needing to be loosened. The church has reformed itself time and again.

To a great extent, we can thank monasteries for preserving languages and cultures, and for promoting learning across Europe. So it should really come as no surprise that Europeans regarded language study, learning, healing and social service as ministry functions when they started to settle North America. It was *déjà vu* all over again.

Thomas King writes off the Franciscans in one sentence on page 151: "Native oral stories from the area tell of Alcatraz as a place where people gathered bird eggs, and as a sanctuary to escape the Franciscan monks, who used Indians in California as slave labour in the building of their missions." If that was true, I am sure the Poverello himself turned over in his grave. There is no substantiation in the book, just innuendo. It does not sound like St Francis.

Jesuits – Ignatius of Loyola, Francis Xavier and several others started this order in 1540. Portuguese explorers had already discovered a new sea route to the Orient by sailing around Africa, and the Americas had been discovered. The aboriginals in America were called "Indians" because it was supposed at first the expeditions had reached India. They had not set out to discover a new continent, they were trying to reach Asia. Thus we now have the West Indies in the

Caribbean and the East Indies between the Pacific and Indian oceans.

An interesting aside is there are 2.6 million indigenous people in the USA today, compared to another 2.7 million immigrants from India and their descendants. I mention this to point out that the small percentage of the population occupied by indigenous people is not what matters most. What matters most is that they are aboriginals. They are our hosts. Missionaries are among their guests.

The Jesuits were a missionary order. This congregation arose from the backlash to the Protestant Reformation called the Counter-Reformation. Jesuit missionaries were well-educated and resourced, because Spain was the super-power of Europe at the time, buoyed up by all the gold it had pillaged in the New World.

But the Jesuits did not set up "monasteries". They set up schools and "missions". One of the founders already arrived in India in 1541 as a missionary. Missions or "mission-stations" have many similarities to the monasteries of old. They are often parked in deep rural areas to provide learning and healing in that place. They became ubiquitous across Africa and America, as monasteries had been across Europe during the Middle Ages.

The church has needed to correct its course at times. For example, when greed crept in, the mendicant orders were founded. Devout Catholics saw through the power and money grab, and called the faithful back to a life of sacrificial service – helping others as opposed to helping themselves. Let's not forget Martin Luther himself started his career as an Augustinian friar. He knew Rome had used unscrupulous means to raise money to expand the Vatican. This triggered the Protestant Reformation in Germany, although there were many other issues as well.

Then came the Counter-Reformation and the founding of the Jesuits. This order has been a huge force in missionary work all over the world. In his chapter on the residential schools debacle, Thomas King writes about two failed experiments in "assimilation". The first one was in 1637, led by a Jesuit missionary Le Jeune. His patron was named Sillery, but the "Catholic Indian village" project failed. The provocateur's morale of this story was, indigenous people were never interested in assimilation. Just in food, temporary shelter and protection from other tribes. (In Africa today, we might say "food-aid, refugee tents and security from militants".) He concludes that people really don't want to convert to Christianity or to go to school, they are not interested in religion or learning. This is not necessarily fatalism. Indigenous people are on a whole different frequency.

But this brings to light a misleading gap in <u>The Inconvenient Indian</u>. What about another Jesuit missionary, Jean de Brébeuf (1593 – 1649)? He was In French Canada concurrently with Le Jeune. He arrived in Quebec City in 1625, and became a missionary to the Wyandot (Huron). Before he was martyred in 1649, he compiled a dictionary of the Huron language and translated a French catechism into the vernacular. This legacy is enormously significant, in so far as the Canadian government has just appointed (in 2021) our first Indigenous Languages Commissioner. Almost 400 years after Brébeuf mastered Wyandot. It's about time!

By this time, John Eliot had already arrived in Boston in 1631 and started to learn the Massachusetts language. He was able to complete a whole Bible translation, which must have been on Brébeuf's mind too, before he was martyred. But the reinterpreter never brings up the positive aspects of missionary work. He dwells on its failures. His second example of failure is the "praying towns" which John Eliot started in the vicinity of Boston. John Eliot was a Puritan, not a Jesuit, but Thomas King regards this as a failed attempt at assimilation of indigenous people into European culture. But really, he is stretching the truth on this one. Europeans had only been settling North America for a few decades by then. They were still hugely outnumbered so the time was not yet ripe for these two social innovations of Le Jeune and

John Eliot. They were visionaries, who are often several steps in front of everyone else.

Pope Francis is a Jesuit. He has been involved in corrective action related to sexual abuse within his own congregation in Europe, the USA and Latin America. More reforms. Sexual impropriety has been linked to celibacy. This was dropped by the Protestant reformers – as were the monasteries. For example, Augustinian monk Martin Luther famously got married and had many children. There does seem to be a disproportionate incidence of sexual transgressions in the Catholic context, compared to other Christian communities? Celibacy also makes it very hard for that church to recruit priests and nuns from the indigenous peoples. And yet, ever since the A-Team and the Desert Fathers, self-denialism has been in the DNA of missionary service.

Sexual abuse is a kind of corruption that needs to be rooted out. Corrupt officials in government must be brought to book, but you don't have to close the whole government. Unless like cancer, it takes over and kills the whole body.

I want to mention two more recent orders...

Christian Brothers – Edmund Rice (1762 – 1844) founded this congregation in Ireland in 1802. It was dedicated to teaching disadvantaged youth. As of 2018, there were 872 Christian Brothers and 172 houses, all over the world.

However, in five countries – including Canada and USA – allegations of sexual abuse arose. Investigations followed and settlements were paid to 700 victims in Canada and 400 in the USA. Governance structures have tried to take corrective action and to cope with the reputation loss. But if the target group was disadvantaged youth, this was double jeopardy. Preying on the poor.

I mention this order because of Thomas King's testimony on page 122. He attended a Christian Brothers high school in California for two years. He didn't like it. Well, as a "missionary kid" I also started my education at a boarding school. It was a primary school, where we spent three months at school then one month at home, in a cycle all through the year. The school was staffed by missionaries, although not Roman Catholic. It was Anglican. I empathize, for it was not an easy row to hoe, although I never suffered abuse. But peer-abuse was hard to control, even though corporal punishment was practiced.

Fall down seven times, get up eight

Ease is a greater threat to progress than hardship

Comboni Fathers - Daniele Comboni (1831 – 1881) was an Italian missionary in Africa. After serving for five years in East Africa, he returned to Italy to found this new order, sometimes called the Verona fathers. It also has an order of nuns called the Comboni Missionary Sisters. In 1867 Comboni opened a missionary training institute in Italy. By the end of 2020, the congregation had 272 houses spread over all five continents, deploying 1,576 religious workers. No less than 1,103 of these were priests.

But allegations of sexual abuse in the 1960s and 1970s arose from young men at a Comboni seminary called St Peter Claver College in England. These were investigated and some corrective action was taken. The victims lament the Comboni order has not shown the same genuine contrition as Pope Francis himself has (in other instances).

I include this order because it has reached down into southern Africa. I got to know a padre who worked in this order in Songo, Mozambique. He was a keeper! Some years later, I visited the Vatican and he gave me a guided tour. He didn't speak English and I don't speak Italian, so the tour was in Portuguese – a language that we both learned to do mission work. So there is a special place in my heart for the Comboni fathers.

If the author's mother sent him to a Christian Brothers school, I will hazard a guess he was brought up with some exposure to Roman Catholicism? Although his profile on Wikipedia makes no mention of his religion. It does say that he self-identifies as being of mixed Cherokee and Greek ancestry. So he might be aware of church efforts to serve indigenous peoples, far and wide. But he only ever mentions the downside. His book is not balanced. Certainly the church has made mistakes, but it has a way of repenting and self-correcting. Failing forward. All I want is for the truth, the *whole truth*, and nothing but the truth (not just unsubstantiated innuendo) about missionaries to be heard.

Any critique of Christian mission work calls for complete, balanced and verifiable facts – to be fair.

4. THE PEREGRINI

A Golden Age of Learning during the Dark Ages of Europe

I am proud of my Irish ancestry, for many reasons. One reason is the Peregrini or "Iona missionary movement". It was enabled by St Columba (521 – 597 AD) who recycled an old monastery on the island of Iona into a Celtic missions training centre.

The deep background to this is the life story of St Patrick, who had evangelized Ireland a century earlier. As a youth, living in Britain, he had been captured by pirates and taken to Ireland to work as a slave. Eventually he escaped and fled on a ship. He spent some time in France, studying to become a priest. Then he felt the call of God on his life to return to Ireland - as a missionary. Where in due course he became known as the Apostle to Ireland.

This period was during the so-called Dark Ages of Europe. The Catholic church continued to dominate from Constantinople, but in western Europe it was sagging. The Patrick-induced revival in Ireland led to the "Golden Age of Learning" of the Celtic church. It still respected the predominance of the Roman church, but its version of

Christianity was highly contextualized. Some Romans including St Boniface (known as the Apostle to the Germans) regarded the Celtic church as heretical. This is because – while it kept close to Roman church theology – its forms of worship were adapted or "contextualized". And church growth was conducted in a relatively unstructured way. It was more mystical than hierarchical.

Then the zealous Celtic church set out to re-evangelize Europe! That is when Columba recycled an Iona monastery into a Celtic missions training centre. He is another patron saint of Ireland along with Patrick himself and Brigit of Kildare.

There are seven distinctive features to the Celtic missionaries. First of all, they did not only come from Ireland, but they were recruited from all over the Celtic world – Scotland, Wales, Cornwall, and Brittany.

Second, they emigrated permanently to their respective mission fields. St Columba settled in Scotland, St Aidan in the north of England, St Willibrord in Frizia (today's Holland), St Columban in today's France and Germany, and St Gall in Switzerland. There was no going back to their Celtic world. In fact, that is why they are called the Peregrini; where they landed, they stayed. No turning back. It is a term used by Romans in the first several centuries AD to describe free citizens of a non-Roman community (i.e. not Latin). Literally, *peregrinus* means "*a foreigner, one from abroad*". They were free to choose, and to go home, but they chose to stay and put down roots in their mission field. We have a similar word in South Africa – *makwerekwere*. It is pejorative. It refers to bird migrations from far away, and it is xenophobic. Labels like this stick and then become normal.

Third, the recruits included aristocrats. These were not mere "monks" but more like ambassadors, who could reach out to the aristocracy in their respective mission fields. Whereas often monks were the sons of poor families that could not afford to raise them, so they were "placed out" in monasteries.

Fourth, there was no hierarchical structure that expected them to report back to headquarters. They had to put down roots in the local economy. In some cases, they had to improvise ways to resource their ministry, although in the case of the aristocrats, they already brought resources with them and even an entourage.

Fifth, they also ordained "wandering bishops" (*episcopi vagantes*) who could deal with diocesan bishops on an equal footing. This reflects the Celtic church's relatively unstructured approach as it tried to engage and fit local culture. This is a bit like project management – in so far as it cuts across the vertical departmentalization of any large firm. To the very organized Romans, this seemed like adhocracy not hierarchy.

Sixth, they were well-educated and devoted to themselves to learning. Illustrated manuscripts were copied and revered. The Book of Kells was a high-water mark, it is still on display. It was created around 800 AD. They did not expect ordinary people to read Latin, so they re-told Bible stories in the vernacular. An account of Creation and the lives of Adam and Eve is one example, in the tenth century Saltair na Rann (Psalter of Quatrains).

Seventh, they tended to establish monasteries as opposed to churches or cathedrals. In rural settings. Thus their approach was one of "brothers" or "mother superiors" more than "fathers". This also helped when it came to self-reliance. This was emulated by later missionary movements. For example, over half of the pioneer missionaries later deployed by the London Missionary Society were the likes of carpenters, traders, farmers, printers and doctors. They could all help with the spiritual outreach, but needed to root themselves in the local economy. They were self-supporting, self-governing and self-propagating.

One of the causes of the Protestant Reformation was the intransigence of the Roman Catholic church, in resisting the tendency of church indigenization. Thus you have Wycliffe and later Tyndale translating the Bible into English, Hus into Czech, Luther into German, Calvin into French, Menno Simons into Dutch and so forth.

The Peregrini were a robust missionary movement that lasted for several centuries and enriched Christian ministry during the Dark Ages. But it started a slow decline after the Synod of Whitby in 664 AD. This was convened to settle a conspicuous clash on the dates of Easter. The Iona missionary movement had kept with the Jewish calendar, to line up Easter with the dates of Passover. This violated a resolution of the Council of Nicea which preferred not to celebrate a key Christian holy day on the same date of the Jewish festival. Iona kept with the pre-Nicea dating while the Roman church calculated the date of Easter the "orthodox" way. This was a convenient way to symbolize some elements of the Celtic church were out of sync with Roman standardization and structure. The Roman church position prevailed at the Synod of Whitby. The Iona movement receded to Iona, taking with it the relics of St Aidan from Northumbria. Priests who had not adhered to the Roman calculation of Easter were replaced, mostly with other Irish priests, who had always adhered to it. Symbolically, this was how Rome dominated, and suppressed indigenization.

Had the Celtic church taken a wrong turn that needed to be corrected? If so, it would not be the first time the church would need to heal itself.

Indigenization would rise again at the time of the Protestant Reformation. And from it would flow once again the missionary zeal to reach the unreached.

There is an interesting sidebar when you think about the Celtic church from the far-flung isles re-evangelizing the continent of Europe. For the name "Celtica" was used by the Greeks and Romans to describe what later was called "Gaul" or even later "France". To secure the road from Italy to Spain along what is now the French Riviera, the Romans provided protection to Massilia (now the city of Marseilles). Roman expansion in the first century BC led to Julius Caesar's campaign, described in his own excellent Latin, in his book <u>The Gallic Wars</u>. He openly relates how he killed over a million Celts (including women and children) and enslaved another million. By his own estimates this was two thirds of the population, but historians think that is exaggerated. It was more likely 16 – 25 percent of the population of Celtica. When you compare this to the percentage of lives lost in World War II (9 percent in

Germany and 14 percent in Russia) you realize how brutal this campaign was.

The three main zones of Celtica were Helvetii (to the east, now Switzerland), Aquitani (to the west) and Belgae (to the north). The Romans occupied this space and Latin soon became the *lingua franca*. What had once been a predominantly Celtic space was now open to immigrations of Visigoths (i.e. Germans) and Franks (around today's Frankfurt) from across the Rhine. It was a major upheaval that some voices call a "genocide". Scholars still debate whether Julius Caesar was a hero, crossing the Rubicon to disrupt the Roman republic and replacing it with the Roman empire? Or was he really the perpetrator of a Celtic genocide? As recently as 2020, a statue of Julius Caesar was defaced and pulled down in Belgium, and some voices have called for the month of July to be re-named! So in a way, it was back to the future - the Peregrini were returning to the Celtic homeland.

St Columba wrote a famous prayer which really captures the motives of the Peregrini: "O Lord, grant us that love which can never die, which will enkindle our lamps but not extinguish them, so that they may shine in us and bring light to others. Most dear Savior, enkindle our lamps that they may shine forever in your temple. May we receive unquenchable light from you so that our darkness will be illuminated and the darkness of the world will be made less. Amen."

As I read The Inconvenient Indian, I was moved by the telling of colonial practice suppressing legitimate and sovereign indigenous tribes and confederacies. They were treated as second-class citizens, or worse yet as sub-humans. As entities like the United States of America and later the Dominion of Canada emerged, those two new nations took the baton from England, France, Holland, Germany and Spain. The 550 indigenous tribes in America and over 600 in Canada were trampled over by the policies of these political entities, time and again. The book's outline of indigenous policy and military involvement in its implementation is comprehensive in scope. But the extent to which the church in general and missionaries in particular are responsible is less convincing.

Revisionists focus on the residential schools debacle to attribute significant responsibility to the church and missionaries across the board. But they ignore their positive contributions in other ways and at other times, that are not easy to reconcile with their assumptions. This can mislead anyone seeking a fair and balanced perspective on the impact of the church and missionaries on indigenous peoples. There was some positive impact, to be fair.

Thomas King is so well informed, and his scoping is so wide, his handling of religious affairs is by comparison incomplete. For example, one of the many photographs sprinkled through the book (on page 90) is of Samuel Worcester - "missionary and defender of Cherokee sovereignty, 19th century". However, there is no mention in the text of his book, who that is or what his role was among the Cherokee. We only hear of three defining court cases – one of which contains his name: *Worcester v. Georgia*. Whereas Tonto - the fictional companion of the Lone Ranger - gets almost two pages of coverage and a full-plate photo. Do Christians get no credit at all for even a dual role in relations? (In part condoning public policy and in part challenging it.) Here is some intel my research captured, to tie up this loose end:

"Samuel Austin Worcester (January 19, 1798 – April 20, 1859), was an American missionary to the Cherokee, translator of the Bible, printer, and defender of the Cherokee sovereignty. He collaborated with Elias Boudinot (Cherokee) in Georgia to establish the *Cherokee Phoenix,* the first Native American newspaper, which was printed in both English and the Cherokee syllabary. The Cherokee gave Worcester the honorary name *A-tse-nu-sti,* which translates to "messenger" in English.

73

"Worcester was arrested in Georgia and convicted for disobeying the state's law restricting white missionaries from living in Cherokee territory without a state license. On appeal, he was the plaintiff in Worcester v. Georgia (1832), a case that went to the United States Supreme Court. The court held that Georgia's law was unconstitutional. Chief Justice John Marshall defined in his *dicta* that the federal government had an exclusive relationship with the Indian nations and recognized the latter's sovereignty, above state laws. Both President Andrew Jackson and Governor George Gilmer ignored the ruling.

"After receiving a pardon from the subsequent governor, Worcester left Georgia on a promise to never return. He moved to Indian Territory in 1836 in the period of Cherokee removal on the Trail of Tears. His wife died there in 1839. Worcester resumed his ministry, and continued translating the Bible into Cherokee. He established the first printing press in that part of the United States, working with the Cherokee to publish their newspaper in Cherokee and English. In 1963, he was inducted into the Hall of Great Westerners of the National Cowboy & Western Heritage Museum."

It seems to me revisionists start with a bias that "Commerce and Christianity" always go hand in hand. I would challenge this assumption. I don't think all Christians or churches always supported the *status quo*. And throughout America's dark ages of white hegemony, there were Christian voices crying in the wilderness against detrimental policy. Like Sam Worcester. But he was not alone, by any means. Why are they ignored by Thomas King and so many others?

Like the vibrant Iona missionary movement at the Synod of Whitby, what are you going to do when Roman hegemony prevails? It would take 900 years before the default-drive predominance of Rome would be challenged again - by the Protestant Reformers.

I am disturbed at this silence. Because the dismantling of the Atlantic Slave Trade ran concurrent to the litany of cruelties and brutalities that Thomas King has catalogued. This reform movement was led by Christians, starting with the Quakers in London, and some principled British MPs like William Wilberforce who introduced the Anti-Slavery Bill in the British Parliament. This trending spread to America where slavery became a huge controversy, leading on to Civil War in the mid-19th century. Typically, Christians fought in both armies. This continues in the war between Russia and the Ukraine – both of which are Christian nations with state churches. I am not condoning this, I am just observing it. Culture war is back on the battlefield. Cultural values can clash between armies that share one and the same faith.

So why don't we get a balanced view? At the risk of sounding too harsh – which I am not – it seems like revisionists are economical with the truth.

It reminds me of a conundrum in the free and democratic South Africa. "Free and democratic", that is - unless you are Khoi or San. These two aboriginal nations used to be called the "Bushmen" or the "Hottentots". The new constitution that has guided South Africa since the 1994 elections won by Nelson Mandela recognizes eleven national languages. Not just the two colonial languages (English and Afrikaans which started as a Dutch creole) but also nine Bantu languages. But not one aboriginal language!

The deep background to this is that the Bantus entered southern Africa overland, on its eastern (Indian Ocean) side. Whereas the Europeans arrived by sea, first at Capetown, seeking a new route to the Orient. I believe the Bantus arrived in this overall space first? Their migrations caused the aboriginals they encountered (and fought) to retreat west into the drier regions towards the Atlantic Ocean. So when the whites arrived, by sea – looking for a route to the Orient - they met the Khoi and the San, who are not "blacks". They are relatively light, short and they speak distinct click languages. By the 21st century, the Khoi have now largely retreated into the Kalahari Desert (now Botswana) and the San into Namibia, an even more inhospitable desert. But there are still some Khoisan inside South Africa along the northern borders with Namibia and Botswana.

They are there, but their languages are not among those enshrined in the "never-again" constitution. Two European languages, nine Bantu languages - but no aboriginal languages. No wonder the Khoisan feel marginalized and miserable. How did the Struggle of blacks against whites get so intense that it overlooked the Khoisan? What does it say about the views that today's black majority hold about the Khoisan? Does this mean institutional racism is still alive and well in South Africa?

I see a parallel between this phenomenon and the way the First Nations – 550 distinct tribes in the United States and over 600 in Canada – were basically side-lined, in spite of a huge struggle over the Atlantic Slave Trade and then slavery inside the USA. Which evolved into the Civil Rights movement and more recently into Black Lives Matter. So if black lives matter, so do red lives or Khoisan lives. The church was at the forefront of the Anti-Slavery movement. But revisionists seem to suggest no Christians or churches ever sympathized with the First Nations, concurrently. This would be inconsistent. I believe a distinction must be made between "Commerce and Christianity" especially at the formative time, way back when North America was largely ruled by business concessions. The prevailing ethos was capitalist greed and not Christian compassion.

At a minimum, I think within the ranks of Christians and churches, there is rarely such a homogenized view. For example, liberation theology is a huge challenge to the conventional alliance of church and state. It emphasizes Christian causes - especially the poor. And it is ready to challenge the *status quo* to champion the powerless.

I once heard a Philipino priest speaking at the University of Zimbabwe. He had spent some time in jail under the Marcos regime for collaborating with the rebels. He never took up arms, but he provided absolution and communion and other Christian care to rebel forces. He was basically a missionary to the rebels.

When Marcos was removed from power, this latter-day Friar Tuck was set free. He was invited by some liberation theologians to speak in Zimbabwe. He explained to us that sometimes life doesn't present us with two choices - good and bad. It is not that clear-cut. He said the two options life presented him with were bad or worse. He knew his choice to go as a missionary to the rebels was unlawful, and thus problematic at best. He was not "doing things right". But to stay and support the Marcos regime he believed would be worse. For Marcos and his cronies were corrupt, despotic, and hazardous to the health of citizens. So instead, he "did the right thing". Even though he knew it was wrong.

I believe missionaries have often had to wash their hands in dirty water. This is not just a visceral issue with me, I have read missionary lore and I know it is true. But this seems to be a blind spot in the dissident narrative.

To the extent that Christians condoned or worse yet participated in the injustices and depravities committed against the First Nations, I join those who have already registered their regrets to those who were injured. As I have expressed my regrets to my African friends for colonialism, slavery and apartheid, and to my Muslim friends for the Crusades. Pope Francis did us proud to come to Canada in 2022 to deliver his regrets.

I ask my Islamic friends if the word "Muslim" really means "submitted to the will of God"? When they confirm it, I tell them - as a Christian missionary - I am also "Muslim". Saying this should not be seen as provocative, but as reaching out. It is cultural relativism, in a world where there is too much polarization caused by cultural hegemony.

5. COLONIAL OUTREACH

Different strokes for different folks

Different European nations have distinctive cultures that go way back. For example, the hotter Mediterranean countries tend to build with masonry while colder northern countries build with wood-frame construction. This could reflect the availability of natural resources for building. Maybe the northern regions were more forested? Or maybe the southern regions were more stony, or deforested from longer centuries of settlement? Maybe there is more marble along the Riviera? Or maybe places like Greece and Rome had accumulated more capital so they could build architecture that would last longer? The Industrial Revolution made England and Germany relatively wealthier, and caused building techniques to adapt? The Eiffel Tower in Paris is a symbol of the advent of steel for building.

As colonies were established all around the world, you could almost tell as you sailed into a port, who had built this city. That's why Macau looks so Portuguese with its ubiquitous tile roofs. That's why Quebec City looks more like France than anywhere else in Canada does. New York started as New Amsterdam and looked much like Holland when it was a colony. Australia and New Zealand had the look and feel of England.

Other trending also affected the colonies. They spoke different languages, and different creoles emerged in different ports of call – depending on which ingredients were mixed in. Out of the Protestant Reformation came Moravian, German, English and later American missionaries. Out of the counter-reformation, the Jesuits (Society of Jesus) emerged. They deployed a force of devout and well-educated missionaries. In Latin America – which still has the look and feel of Spain – a theology of liberation emerged. It became a force in challenging the prevalence of capitalism – brought to you by colonialism.

I have travelled more than once along the St Lawrence River in Quebec. Its old seigneurial system can still be seen as well as the stone houses – so different from the log and frame construction of Upper Canada, built on square plots of land. A very French atmosphere. Before Quebec's rapid secularization, it was predominantly Roman Catholic – like France. Every village you come to has a huge church with a steeple at the centre of town. Back in the days when it was a French colony, there would be few if any Protestants in Quebec. Although in recent decades, Protestant churches have been planted there. The question is always whether priests were the change agents or did they collaborate with the *status quo*?

In Lower Canada (i.e. Quebec) as in so many places, on other continents, hospitals and schools were often established and run by the church. In Quebec and to a lesser extent in western Canada, healing and learning were first established at mission stations. For example, Misericordia Hospital right in today's downtown Winnipeg, Manitoba, has Roman Catholic roots.

Quebec is quite a contrast to the English colonies. So many of them were populated by Christians who came to the "New World" to get away from the clashes between religions or denominations. Especially in England, where the rivalry was militant – that is, until Henry VIII nationalized the church. And after the Church of England emerged, between it and the "non-conformists".

This freedom of religion manifests itself in urban planning and architecture. Of course there were exceptions, like Maryland, which was settled predominantly by Roman Catholics. But pluralism was the order of the day, so it is still very common to find four different churches standing where two streets cross. On each corner stands one church – St George's Episcopal (English), Knox Presbyterian (Scottish or Dutch), St Peter's Roman Catholic (Italian or Irish), and First

Baptist. This would have been anathema in Lower Canada (Quebec), but it reflects the different policies of European empires in their respective colonies.

So mission work in North America was a potpourri. There were monasteries, holy orders, mission stations, schools and clinics, an abundance of churches, orphanages, linguists, Bible translators, evangelists and seminaries. Some of the most prestigious ivy-league universities today started as seminaries. In fact the culture of philanthropy really took off in this new mix. One French observer, Alexis de Tocqueville, travelled in America in the 1830s and thereafter wrote about American democracy. He was processing why the French Revolution had sputtered out, overtaken by Napoleon. Compared to American democracy, which took off. One of his observations was the prominent role of community participation in nonprofits. Combining religious and altruistic motives, this third sector (i.e. non-government and nonprofit) gave a huge surge to democratic development in the New World.

I have also traveled extensively in South Africa - where there are similarities and differences. Originally, the Cape colony was Dutch. But as the Dutch fought the English in various wars, Capetown would fly the Dutch flag at times and the English flag at other times. This went on for over a century. When Jan van Riebeeck was appointed to colonize

Capetown, it was upgraded from being a mere provisioning stop-over port en route to the Orient. It became a full-fledged colony. This naturally attracted missionaries from both Holland and England. Even today the Anglican cathedral of South Africa is in Capetown, the "mother city". But the Dutch Reformed church really came to dominate the landscape of the interior, as the country evolved into the Union of South Africa.

In the early days, Christian outreach in South Africa followed the same pathways as elsewhere – mission stations, language study, Bible translation, schools and hospitals, etc. A Moravian mission (from Czechia) was already functioning in the Cape when the London Missionary Society first sent Dutch and British missionaries to the Cape. The LMS went on to establish mission stations far into the interior and beyond the boundaries of the Cape colony.

But in South Africa, the term "missionary" gradually developed a new and different connotation. This is because later settlement by Europeans happened on a much more massive scale. In fact, South Africa started to look pretty much like any country in Europe or America, in terms of infrastructure and urban planning.

In their own way, the "Boers" or farmers were - and still are - deeply religious. So every town that sprung up built a church with a steeple (similar to the skyline in Quebec). All the Boer farmers attended these Dutch Reformed churches and from time to time, they were each visited by their pastor. That is, the man who preached on Sundays in their (white) church – to them. In their farm homes, the Boers typically kept a "parson's lounge" – used only on these visits. Otherwise, they lived their day-to-day life in the farm kitchen.

But every Dutch Reformed church also had a "missionary". Another man, whose role was to evangelize "the blacks". When the pastor halted his horse and buggy in front of the Boer's house on a pastoral visit, he was always accompanied by another white man, who would not go into the farmer's house, but would rather meet with all the black farm workers, out back. To minister to them.

You can give some credit to other mission efforts too. They operated in the same manner as all African countries (reaching out to blacks where they lived, around their mission stations). But in South Africa, it was different - black people were also reached where they worked. (Not all blacks worked on Boer farms, so one approach or the other reached them.) White people went to church and every local church supported a "missionary" as well as a pastor. To a very great extent, this paradigm made South Africa a place where God is worshipped widely. By all races.

Yet there are still distinct cultures. Christianizing South Africa has not erased tribal identities and their own languages. You can be a Zulu and a Christian. There are so many Zulu Christians, the Zulus could be another Christian nation.

There was a yeast in Bible teaching that did not rise at first. But all that teaching to black farm workers eventually had a subversive effect. They wanted to read the Bible, and that meant learning how to read. There was always this implicit risk – in evangelism, in language study, in literacy training, in education. Willem Saayman writes of "chickens coming home to roost", in his book <u>Christian Mission in South Africa</u>.

Much later, in 1977, an African-American preacher called Leon Sullivan of the Zion Baptist church (in Philadelphia) introduced a list of principles that American companies operating in South Africa could use to ratchet up the pressure against apartheid. Because by law, up until that time, blacks were unable to hold supervisory positions in the work place. This was getting to be un-sustainable, and the corporate sector realized it. By the 1980s, that yeast started to rise in the Sullivan Code. Before long, and with a boost from sanctions, political prisoners like Nelson Mandela and the "treason trialists" were released and free and democratic elections were held. All the while, both blacks and whites attend church in droves. The Zionist church (almost all black) is now the biggest church denomination in South Africa. On its Easter pilgrimage to Mount Moria in Limpopo province, it can mobilize over one million worshippers!

Going back two hundred years... Twenty years after the British secured a permanent stay in the Cape Colony, the Boers or "Afrikaners" organized the "Great Trek". This took them across the Vaal River which was the northern boundary of the Cape Colony. Into the "Transvaal", where they set up a number of Boer Republics. One of these was the Orange Free State, the colour orange, of course, connoting a loyalty to Holland, the Duke of Orange, and all that. The Dutch soccer team still dresses in orange uniforms at the World Cup! Without going into detail, the Boers had developed a manifesto to recruit people to join the Great Trek. It had twenty points, one of which was they took exception to the egalitarian way that missionaries treated indigenous people.

My reading of history is that, more often than not, missionaries were the champions who defended the rights of indigenous people. Immediately upon his arrival in Capetown in 1799, before venturing inland, Dr Johannes

Van der Kemp visited the clergy in the city who owned slaves – and rebuked them! The LMS soon started a church in Capetown, which was open to non-whites as well as whites.

This distinction and tension between Commerce and Christianity cannot be overstated. Dr Van der Kemp trekked right across the Cape to the kraal of Gaika, king of the Xhosa. This was a black tribe, living outside the boundaries of the Cape colony – to the east. (Not the Khoisan of the western Cape, but Bantu.) It is clear from Dr Van der Kemp's memoirs that the indigenous people of the Cape colony were originally Khoi and San – not Bantus. Whereas the Xhosa were and are one of the five Nguni tribes, along with the Zulus, Swazis, Ndebeles and Xangans – as you move northwards along the eastern border of South Africa and on into Mozambique.

There were high levels of instability around the eastern border of the Cape colony, which was the Fish River. Dr Van der Kemp tried to learn the Xhosa language to be able to assist the Xhosa with Bible translation and literacy, as well as his medical skills. But he was harassed repeatedly by Boer settlers. His life was in constant danger.

Because of the volatility, he was recalled back inside the colony's borders by the Cape governor. Here is an account of what happened in the church of Graaff Reinet when he chose to settle there, just back inside the colony. He agreed to pastor the settlers' church on the proviso that it be open to both whites and indigenous people. In his inaugural sermon, Dr Van der Kemp preached from Psalm 74. His words would have made Martin Luther King applaud. According to his biographer Sarah Gertrude Millin (on page 243 of The Burning Man), he called out the Boers for not worshipping together with non-whites:

"The enemy hath done wickedly in the sanctuary. Thine enemies roar in the midst of thy congregations... They have cast fire into the sanctuary, they have defiled the dwelling place of thy name."

The toast hit the floor, marmalade-side-down! The Boer settlers wrote to Capetown, saying if the missionaries and their indigenous followers were not out of Graaff Reinet within three months, no threat of superior force would stop them from attacking the English. "Nor will it be as last time. We begin to prepare forthwith."

Clearly, the further you got into the interior, the less the British could enforce their relatively liberal policies on Boer settlers. It was Commerce *versus* Christianity. This distinction is missing in The Inconvenient Indian.

Thomas King has a blind spot in his book. He cannot make this distinction between pro-poor missionary work and "organized religion". The two were often at odds with one another, and if the priests condoned slavery or exploitation, the monks and nuns opposed it – like Friar Tuck. They were ready to rob from the rich to give to the poor, so to speak. Their outreach went hand in hand with proselytization, I know. I don't have a problem with that. Jesus did it. He healed the sick and cast out demons while recruiting and training his own cadres. His A-Team did it, in spite of violent opposition. For their leader had told them to go into all the world and make disciples. They followed his example...

The book outlines the two pathways of extermination and assimilation. These two options played out on other continents as well, not only in North America. He writes on page 110: "extermination was also seen as an expression of "natural law", a concept conceived by Aristotle in the fourth century BC and used by the Spanish humanist Juan de Sepulveda in the sixteenth as a legal justification for the enslavement of Native people..."

That's the same guy who lost the great debate in 1550 to Dominican friar Bortolome de las Casas, as outlined above. So not all Europeans agreed on the correctness of Aristotle's analysis, which was a bit out of date even in the mid-16th century! Especially when it collided head-on with the teachings of Jesus. Then Thomas King adds something that is hugely understated in his book:

90

"In the minds of many, these were not so much cruelties as they were variations on the principles underlying the concept "survival of the fittest", a phrase that Herbert Spencer had fashioned in 1864 and that would become synonymous with Charles Darwin's theory of natural selection."

That's all that is ever said about Charles Darwin, who published The Origin of Species in 1859. It went viral, as we say today. This line of thinking rapidly became very influential. It is often called "social Darwinism" and is regarded as one of three sects of overall humanism. In his prize-winning book Sapiens, historian Noah Yuval Harari, describes liberalism, socialism and evolutionary humanism, on pages 257 and 258. Here are some excerpts:

"The **liberal** belief in the free and sacred nature of each individual is a direct legacy of the traditional Christian belief in free and eternal individual souls. Humanists believe that the unique nature of *Homo sapiens* is the most important thing in the world, and it determines the meaning of everything that happens in the universe. The supreme good is the good of *Homo sapiens*.

"Like liberal humanism, **socialist** humanism is built on monotheist foundations. The idea that all humans are created equal is a revamped version of the monotheist conviction that all souls are equal before God. Socialists believe that 'humanity' is collective rather than individualistic. They hold as sacred not the inner voice of each individual, but the species *Homo sapiens* as a whole. Whereas liberal humanism seeks as much freedom as possible for individual humans, socialist humanism seeks equality between all humans.

"The only humanist sect that has actually broken loose from traditional monotheism is **evolutionary humanism**, whose most famous representatives are the Nazis. What distinguished the Nazis from other humanist sects was a different definition of 'humanity', one deeply influenced by the theory of evolution. In contrast to other humanists, the Nazis believed that humankind is not something universal and eternal, but rather a mutable species that can evolve or degenerate. Man can evolve into superman, or degenerate into a subhuman."

I agree with Harari. So from the year Darwin published <u>The Origin of Species</u> until the Nazis were defeated in 1945, social Darwinism was in the ascendancy. It was hugely influential. I would lay the blame for the corruption of assimilation – the prevalent government policy in North America - on Darwin, not on Jesus. Thomas King is right about one thing – at times it was hard to tell extermination (a k a annihilation) and assimilation apart.

But it was not the best-selling book of its century. In 1867, Karl Marx published Das Kapital. "Soft socialism" hardened into Marxism. It comes in different shades like Marxist-Leninism, Maoism and Fanonism (most popular in Africa). The USA was and is so ensconced in capitalism, this became the handbook for America's enemies. It sold better outside America. But it was not the best-seller of its century either.

In 1879, Henry George published Progress and Poverty. He was an American pastor, and his book outsold Darwin and Marx in its century, even though it was the last of the three to be published. He had a huge influence on reformers like Tolstoy in Russia before the Bolshevik revolution, Franklin Delano Roosevelt in the USA and Tommy Douglas in Canada.

But guess what? His book was out-sold in the 19th century by only one other book. The Bible.

The first residential school in Canada started in 1840. By 1932 there were more than eighty. This is the period that social Darwinism emerged and took off like a rocket.

Carlisle Indian Industrial School in Pennsylvania was the first American institution of its kind. It opened in 1879. By 1909 there were 25 such schools; plus 157 on-reservation boarding schools; plus 307 days schools.

The timing is so obvious, I don't know why Thomas King plays it down. Books like The Origin of Species and Das Kapital did not come out of the church. Christians were still busy translating the Bible into dozens of indigenous languages. But it is not cool to blame Darwin or Marx for atrocities. From the detrimental policies of Lenin and Stalin probably 30 million Russian peasants starved to death. Not to mention the killing fields of Asia. And the loss of 56 million lives in World War II combat, to defeat Nazi aggression. Not to mention the Holocaust which took another six million Jewish lives.

The way I read it, this is not just an oversight by the author. It is not a gap in his understanding. It is intentionally understated. Because in academic circles at the time his book was published, revisionism was in the ascendancy. Social Darwinism was the proverbial elephant in the room that revisionists don't want to talk about. It better suits their agenda to blame Christianity.

It is hard to define what wokeism is, because it has many strands. The lowest common denominator seems to be to wake up to what has really been going on – while you were sleeping. The Inconvenient Indian lines up with this trending, broadly speaking. But this is a good place to mention that among the strands of woke ideologies are humanism, Marxism and Black Lives Matter. And others. It is a coalition of diverse Leftists who have a massive change agenda. Thomas King is riding this wave. Needless to say, on the whole, woke-induced revisionism is against religion in general and Christianity in particular. This is not to say that there are no leftist Christians, there are. But there are no atheist Christians. That is oxymoron. And secular religions that deny God are at the forefront of revisionism.

6. MODERN MISSIONARY MOVEMENT

Climb every mountain, ford every stream...

Three archetypes are described in <u>The Inconvenient Indian</u> - blood-thirsty savage, the noble savage and the dying savage. This got me thinking...

Hollywood motion pictures use a success formula that is purposed to keep viewers coming back. One thing they do is to reflect back to movie-goers their commonly-held beliefs and convictions. Rarely are movies made to challenge our assumptions or prevailing views. Instead, they parrot opinions back to us, reinforcing what we already believe. So in a similar vein, I can think of three archetypes of missionaries:

a) Those with patronizing attitudes or a superiority complex, which amounts to cultural hegemony. They regard indigenous people as "uncivilized". A great example of this are the missionaries in the 1966 motion picture <u>Hawaii</u>.

b) The humble servants whose sensitivity to local customs amounts to cultural relativism. They have a high view of the natives, regarding them as peers who still live in an

Eden-like stage of innocence. A great example of this are the missionaries in the 1986 motion picture The Mission.

c) The pioneer missionary who is tossed to and fro, back and forth, between larger forces beyond their control - like war, disasters, population migration and economic expansion. A great example of this is Father LaForgue, a Jesuit priest in the 1991 motion picture Black Robe.

If you take these three motion pictures as a small sampling of prevailing views about missionaries, you would suppose preconceptions were improving slowly (between 1966 and 1991). One could begin to make a distinction between the greedy exploitation of colonialism and the pro-poor views of missionaries. But all that changed with a wave of serious disclosures about residential schools…

We need to bear the calendar in mind. Residential schools were instituted fairly late in the narrative of North America's occupation by Europeans. The period under review by the Truth and Reconciliation Commission (TRC) in Canada was from the 1880s to the 1990s. Bear in mind the dates of the three missionary archetypes outlined above are 1634 in Black Robe, the 1750s in The Mission and the 1820s in Hawaii (a movie made from James Michener's book of the same name). So the residential schools debacle is relatively recent compared to the pioneering efforts of missionaries like Father LaForgue, Father Gabriel and Rev. Abner Hale.

This brings up another interesting sequence – possibly a gradual degeneration of the high ideals of early pioneer mission work, to a later phase after America and Canada became independent nations and started themselves to send out their own workers to the mission frontiers. For example, Rev Abner Hale was an American pastor, trained at the Yale Divinity School and sent to an island that eventually became one of the United States in 1959. Could it be not just our perceptions changed over time, but missionaries themselves also changed? One way or another, are we shooting at a moving target? It seems to me there may have been some Abner Hales (not all) in the residential schools system, mixed with some LaForgues. Concurrent to many Gabriels out there in the real world of missionary work. But certainly the residential schools debacle has tarnished the image of Christianity, the church and missionaries.

Is it just guilt by association that grows stronger as colonialism gained momentum? From the Age of Discovery to the Age of Exploration, and on to the Age of Domination? That last words rings so close to "dominion", as in the Dominion of Canada. Its confederation was in 1867. Residential schools were only launched in the 1880s.

On pages 40 and 41 of his book, Thomas King writes: "What we watched on the screen over and over was the implicit and inevitable acquiescence of Native people to Christianity and Commerce. No matter what happened, the question that was asked and answered again and again on the silver screen was: Can Indians survive in a modern world? And the answer, even in sympathetic films such as *Broken Arrow, Little Big Man,* and *Dances With Wolves* was always: No."

There you have it – "Christianity and Commerce". Tarred with the same brush. But a nuance was missing, and I will unpack a few samples from the annals of missionary history (not just fiction or films), to show a distinction must be made between "Christianity and Commerce".

The Moravians

One of the rising stars of the Protestant Reformation was John Hus. He was from what we now call Czechia, and travelled to England to study under John Wycliffe. Revival followed his return to Czechia, and of course Hus was a great influence on other reformers, including Martin Luther in Germany. A native of Bohemia (now a province of Czechia), Hus opposed certain Church doctrines and practices, and as a consequence was martyred. His blood was a seed...

The Moravian Mission was the first entity to send missionaries to South Africa. Moravia is another province of Czechia. As far back as 1737, Georg Schmidt established a mission station called Genadendal (i.e. the Valley of Grace) near Capetown. However, neither the settlers nor the predominant Dutch Reformed church could abide the radical views of the Moravians, so Schmidt was forced to leave. Christianity *versus* Commerce.

The Cape colony change hands several times in the run-up to Napoleon's defeat at the battle of Trafalgar (Holland was allied to France). This affected missionaries, as English governors tended to be more liberal than Dutch. So in 1792, the Moravians were allowed to return. They found the remnant of the first Moravian congregation was still active, and they rebuilt the mission station. The Moravian church deployed missionaries all across the Cape "from sea even unto sea" (Atlantic to Indian in this case). They were not stooges of imperialism.

London Missionary Society

Somehow I have a special affinity to Johannes Van der Kemp, the Dutch physician (trained in Edinburgh) who led the first LMS team to South Africa in 1799. I enjoyed reading accounts of his life and times, published as The Burning Man. These were based on a careful study of his personal diary by the author – Sarah Gertrude Millin. One has to tolerate references to "Hottentots" and "kaffirs" which were not yet considered insensitive at the time of the book's publication in 1952.

Early on, Van der Kemp visited the Moravian mission station to observe it. He then traveled with a guide right across the Cape to Gaika's kraal, as outlined above. He was then recalled back into the Cape Colony for his own security, but it did not go well for him in Graaff Reinet. So he moved again, and again, landing finally at a mission station called Bethelsdorp (near present-day Nelson Mandela Bay).

The sites granted for LMS mission stations kept getting moved to poorer and poorer quality farmland. Nevertheless, he learned to speak the Khoi language fluently and worked away at Bible translation and literacy training. These three always went hand-in-hand. This affinity with the Khoi meant he was kept informed by whistle-blowers of wrongs and ferocities being committed by Boer farmers against the indigenous people. He recorded these and sent them to the governor of the Cape colony and to a British MP called William Wilberforce. This Christian leader was at the forefront of the evangelical lobby against slavery. The evangelical press in Britain was full of reports coming in from South Africa, and this had a major influence on public opinion – against the Atlantic Slave Trade. The Anti-Slavery Bill was introduced in British parliament by Wilberforce soon after this.

When British forces defeated Napoleon at the battle of Trafalgar, Capetown was flying a Dutch flag. A sea battle near Capetown ensued in 1806. The English were victorious. Dutch governor Jan Willem Janssens was replaced by Britain's Lord Caledon. The new governor listened to Dr Van der Kemp's litany of iniquities, about the way that settlers (Dutch, British, Portuguese, *et alia*) were treating the Khoi and the San inhabitants of the western Cape. Lord Caledon thus appointed a commissioner Colonel Collins to visit the LMS mission station at Bethelsdorp. When Collins returned to Capetown in 1809, he recommended the mission be closed on the grounds that it existed "not to benefit the Colony, but the Hottentots". To his credit, Caledon did not do so.

Then in 1811, Lord Caledon was replaced by Sir John Craddock as governor. In the interim, the LMS whistle-blowing had reached shrill proportions in England. So upon his arrival, Craddock appointed a circuit court to investigate the abominations. In 1812, the "Black Circuit" brought a total of fifty-seven white women and men to trial. One thousand Khoi, European and Xhosa witnesses were called. Several defendants were found guilty and punished. This really brings to light a huge distinction between Commerce and Christianity.

On its bicentenary in 1999, the LMS published a book called On the Missionary Trail, derived from archives of its pioneer era. I have cherry-picked a bit more evidence from researcher Tom Hiney's findings to strengthen my case...

The LMS sent some missionaries to Guyana in South America. One Dutch landowner named Hermanus Hilbertus Post asked for a missionary to preach to his slaves and to teach them – at his plantation called Le Resouvenir. The LMS deployed a missionary named John Wray. In 1808, Bethel Chapel was opened on Post's plantation. It soon had a mixed-race congregation of 600.

Inspired by this initial success, landowner Post applied to the governor, Lord Bentinck, to open a second chapel in the capital, Georgetown. This was refused, but he was allowed to open a school for slaves. The LMS deployed Rev John Davies to run the school. Despite British sentiment against slavery, Governor Bentinck did not want to see it come to an end. So when the landowner died in 1811, Bentinck closed down the slave school and issued a proclamation that no more than twenty slaves could assemble in one place, undermining the two churches.

Missionary John Wray left Guyana in haste to inform MP William Wilberforce in person. He had to sleep on top of cotton bales on the deck of a ship to cross the Atlantic! Wilberforce took the matter to Parliament, where Bentinck's proclamation was declared to be illegal.

William Carey was deployed to India. Tom Hiney writes (on page 20): "The stubbornness of the people towards a new religion ... was matched only by the hostility of the British East India Company. Missionaries had been banned in British India before 1813. Many colonials simply did not want them there and thought the very idea of sending them was 'pernicious, imprudent, useless, dangerous, profitless, and fantastic. It strikes against all reason and sound policy and brings the peace and safety of our possessions into peril'. Carey was forced to settle his Baptist mission in the tiny Danish river enclave of Serampore in Bengal. Here he pursued his Bengali translation of the New Testament...

Tom Hiney continues: "The three missionaries were also busy collecting evidence about the Hindu rite of suttee - the burning (alive) of a dead man's widow. Carey had witnessed suttee first in 1799... In 1813, when the East India company's powers came up for parliamentary renewal in

London, it was debated whether to remove the ban on missionaries. During the debate the pro-missionary MP William Wilberforce read to the House Joshua Marshman's account of a suttee ritual...

"The three Baptists had collected evidence of 300 suttees which had taken place in only six months within thirty miles of Calcutta. Thanks in large part to their detailed reports, Wilberforce and the Evangelical lobby won the debate and from 1813 Christian mission work in British India was legalized."

There are many tales of other pioneer missionaries in places like Tahiti and China in Hiney's book <u>On the Missionary Trail</u>. In Tahiti, infanticide was practiced and in China, foot-binding of young girls was the norm. This put women in a position of perpetual disadvantage. I do not regard this as subversive undermining of local practice by cultural hegemony. Especially when the missionaries were busy with language study, Bible translation, literacy, learning and healing. There was no UN charter on the rights of the child, no Bill of Rights to counter these cruel customs that harmed women. This was not civilization versus savagism. It was liberation ministry - and it was beneficial to the poor.

From sea even unto sea

I cannot conclude unpacking evidence to support my contentions without mentioning two great mission stations in Canada – the Grenfell Mission in Labrador and the Bella Bella Mission in British Columbia. Between the Atlantic and the Pacific, countless citations of evidence could be made. So the wide geography of these two missions is symbolic of this tiny sampling.

One hundred and thirty years ago, in 1892, British surgeon and medical missionary Dr Wilfred T Grenfell arrived in Newfoundland. He started a coastal mission reaching far north to Labrador. He became a living legend, like Dr David Livingstone before him (an LMS deployee) and Dr Albert Schweitzer after him.

The mission hospital that Dr Grenfell built at Battle Harbour on the Labrador coast grew and attracted many young doctors. His mission also sailed ships up and down the coast as mobile clinics to very remote communities. The Grenfell Mission was like a spiritual lighthouse on the Atlantic coast of Canada. Dr Grenfell became a popular motivational speaker in Canada, the USA and Britain. He was knighted in 1927. He attracted unpaid youth volunteers every summer from all over Canada, the USA and Britain to add value to the ministry.

Institutional arrangements had to be adapted to keep up with the scale of Dr Grenfell's ambitions. Long after Dr Grenfell's death in 1940, a second hospital was built in St Anthony in 1968. In due course, these hospitals were absorbed into the Province of Newfoundland's health care network. So they are now run by the government and the Grenfell missions in Canada, the USA and Britain now fund coastal projects. Over $40 million has been disbursed to over one thousand projects.

According to the International Grenfell Association's website, Dr Grenfell "possessed a profound Christian faith and believed that a vital part of his mission was also to spread the Word of God and attend to the spiritual needs of those living on the coast."

Meanwhile on the west coast of Canada, another mission hospital was begun by the Methodist church. It was an outreach project to Japanese fisherman, starting in 1896. They sailed along coastal British Columbia until the internment of Japanese in Canada, in 1942. There was already a cannery operating at Steveston, showing again that business interests were normally concurrent to missionary activity.

At first, starting in 1898, Dr R W Large was deployed at the island hospital during summers only. Then in 1900 he was deployed full-time. Dr Large worked there until 1906 when he went to work at Rivers Inlet Hospital in Ocean Falls. In 1910, he transferred to the Mission Hospital in Port Simpson. The R W Large Memorial Hospital in Bella Bella was named in his memory after his death in 1920.

As it happens, my father served for a year at the Bella Bella hospital in 1948. This was his first job as a doctor after graduating from University of Toronto medical school. After that, he headed to the Belgian Congo as a medical missionary, where he built *Taraja* mission hospital near Bunia. That is where I was born and raised – as a "mish kid". My father remained active in missions all his life, and was awarded the Order of Canada for humanitarian service.

It would be very hard to catalogue all the mission work in learning and healing that has taken place all around the world over the past two centuries. It has been astounding. However, as governments have gradually taken over mission schools and hospitals during this same period, there are fewer living legends today than there were in the heyday of Dr Johannes Van der Kemp, Dr David Livingstone, Dr Wilfred Grenfell, Dr Richard Large and Dr Albert Schweitzer.

But they did not get everything quite right, especially as government policy crept into institutional policies and procedures, preceded by the dramatic rise in evolutionary humanism. For example, the Bella Bella hospital – after the death of Dr Large – was reported for its involvement in the involuntary sterilization of local people from the Heiltsuk Nation. Including women and children. Eye witness accounts from human rights trials detail how Dr George Darby, a United church missionary doctor, sterilized non-Christian peoples of Native descent between 1928 and 1962 at the R W Large Memorial Hospital.

I cannot imagine medical missionaries at a church hospital would get involved in such unethical practices. However, government policy can be detrimental and there is no question that social Darwinism became a force to be reckoned with in the first half of the twentieth century. I am not excusing or condoning involuntary sterilization. But it fits the narrative of government policy better than the hospital's mission roots. Remembering the founder Dr R W Large was also a Methodist minister.

In the 21st century, there are an increasing number of moral and medical challenges facing the church and medical missions. We should remember compliance with government policy can get us into hot water. But then again, so can non-compliance! I can only wonder how much of a force evolutionary humanism still is in a world that has lost its monotheistic foundations? Doing the Lord's work on

Caesar's dime could be riskier than ever. When the church, in its mission, is guided by the government, it will fail twice – in terms of church outreach and as an instrument of government.

The Missionary Teenager

One of Canada's greatest evangelists and missions advocates was Oswald J Smith, who founded The Peoples Church in Toronto. This church has distinguished itself by supporting missionary outreach all over the world, in a big way. "OJ" preached all over the world before Billy Graham launched his better-remembered efforts.

One of OJ's grandsons is a close friend of mine. He shared with me that his grandfather served as a missionary before going on to study at the Manitoba College, Toronto Bible College and McCormick Theological Seminary in Chicago. When OJ served as an itinerant worker of the Bible Society and the Methodist church in 1908-09 along the west coast of British Columbia, he was still a teenager! He sold Bibles and preached – including at the Bella Bella mission. On page 29 of his autobiography, The Story of My Life, he writes: "Arriving at Bella Bella, I preached for Dr Large, a medical missionary, sold many Bibles to the Indians, and then boarded the *Camosun* for Alert Bay. We were detained by a heavy fog and arrived at midnight."

OJ was invited to fill in as pastor of the church and schoolteacher in Hartley Bay, an indigenous settlement, during the winter of 1908 - 09. I have selected three paragraphs from his autobiography from pages 31, 32 and 34:

"Never will I forget that first night. Oh, how lonely it was! I was the only white person on the reserve. I shivered in my bed. As I lay there it dawned upon me with terrible force that I was alone among the Indians. For a long time I lay awake. Every sound startled me, and I listened, almost afraid to move. At last I fell asleep, but awakened several times during the night. I was now nineteen.

"Four times each week I preached to the Indians. They nearly all attended. God was with us and abundantly blessed, making our hearts to glow with joy. During the week I taught school, having the unique experience of teaching Indian children.

"Often I look back and wonder how I ever did it. I think of my two sons, Glen and Paul, when they were nineteen, and to imagine them in a similar position makes me shiver. Certainly I was far too young to be roughing it among Indians and construction men more than three thousand miles from home. Sin abounded on every side. I was in constant danger. But God watched over me and brought me safely through. Blessed be His Name!"

I once had the privilege to meet OJ when he was about the age I am now, in his home in Toronto. Accompanied by his grandson who I went to school with. The Peoples Church and its outreach is his legacy, as are his books. And, of course, his progeny; an Africa proverb says "The fruit never falls far from the tree."

7. MISSIONS, LANGUAGE AND LEARNING

Language study → *Bible translation* → *Literacy* → *Education*

Many monasteries were closed by the Protestant reformers, giving rise to alternate ways of assisting the poor. For example, the closing of the monasteries in Germany led to the streets of its cities filling up with vagabond children. This caused Auguste Francke to establish the first "Ragged School" in Halle, Germany, in 1695. Before long this became a new model for orphan care. It was transplanted to Britain by a German pietist named George Muller in 1834. In 1852, Lord Shaftsbury's Ragged School Union in the UK. In 1868, Dr Barnardo launched his Juvenile Mission in east London.

As orphanages gave way to fostering and adoption as the strategy of choice in the 20th century, many Barnardo orphans were "placed out" in Canada. I had the privilege to get to know one well, in the late 20th century. He had been among the first to be placed out, instead of in an orphanage. He survived many challenges but went on to own his own farm, where he fostered some indigenous orphans. It is important to note that social innovation kept finding new and better solutions for orphan care. Not for indigenous children in particular, but for all orphans. In the 19th century alone, there was a deluge of orphans, caused by famine in Ireland and the American Civil War. In the 20th century, there were more war orphans and then AIDS orphans as well. There are relatively few Covid orphans.

In 1729, the first-ever American orphanage opened in New Orleans. In 1825, there were only two orphanages in New York State – but by 1866 there were sixty! In 1854, Charles Loring Brace, head of the Children's Aid Society, sent out the first Orphan Train from New York City. Researchers estimate from 150,000 to 400,000 children were "placed out" on orphan trains, perhaps as many as 100,000 in Missouri alone. In 1859, Pennsylvania's soldier's orphans' schools were established. The number of American orphans increased by 300 percent during and after the Civil War.

We must be honest about how this rolled out. First of all, learning had been embedded in monasticism for centuries. That is where the Bible was copied and translated and literacy was taught. These functions are symbiotic. But there was music too, drama and other literature – classical and in the vernacular. Then came the traumatic closing of the monasteries in northern Europe. This resulted in new solutions for learning being invented – like the Ragged

School which is synonymous with the orphanage. Social innovation.

But a Moravian Brethren bishop - John Amos Comenius (1592 – 1670) - came up with an even more innovative and comprehensive solution to education. He was perhaps the earliest proponent of universal education. This was a century before the Industrial Revolution, so the challenge to Comenius was not how to upgrade the basic education of the work force. This philosopher, theologian and pedagogue – out of what is now Czechia – simply wanted people to have a better quality of life. This was Jan Hus country (Protestant Reformer 1369 – 1415). So Comenius also wanted everyone to read the Bible for themselves. Because print-technology was now all the rage thanks to Johannes Gutenburg who had died in 1458. So ordinary people could now buy books. Comenius was a social innovator of note. He introduced the "curriculum" and the "textbook". His influence cannot be understated – he is often called the father of modern education. He was in demand all over Europe, advising governments how to launch this new approach. - the school.

By the time Comenius died in 1670, several colonies had already been established in North America, starting with the founding of Quebec City in 1608 (by the French) and Massachusetts in 1620 (by the Pilgrim Fathers). Then in 1652 Jan van Riebeeck had established a definitive Dutch colony at Capetown. Before long, Comenius' new trending in education was exported to the colonies. His approach to education eventually reached German colonies like Pennsylvania and thence even Upper Canada (now the province of Ontario). It came to prevail as the model for mass education.

Concurrent with Comenius, far across the Atlantic, the Bible was translated into Wampanoag or "Massachusett" language (Algonquin family). This was the first Bible translation into any North American indigenous language. As outlined above, John Eliot began his Natick version in 1653 and finished it in 1661-63, with a revised edition in 1680-85. It was the first Bible to be printed in North America.

Since then, it has been translated in whole or in part into dozens of Native languages. Wikipedia provides the following data on Bible translation into Native American languages. I have cherry-picked 67 of them by date:

Year	Language	Bible translation
1821	Delaware/Lenape	Four Gospels
1824	Cherokee	Gospel of John
1830	Abenaki	Gospel of Mark
1833	Ojibwa	Whole Bible
1836	Mohawk	New Testament
1840	Aluet	Gospel of Matthew
1843	Dakota/Lekota	Luke and John
1843	Iowa	Gospel of Matthew
1844	Potawatomi	Mark and Book of Acts
1845	Nez Perce	Gospel of Matthew
1848	Choctaw	New Testament
1848	Sugpiaq/Alutiiq	Gospel of Matthew
1862	Plains Cree	Whole Bible
1870	Malecite-Passamaquoddy	Gospel of John
1871	Micmac	New Testament

1874	Seneca	Four Gospels
1876	Moose Cree	New Testament
1878	Dene Suline/Chipewyan	Four Gospels
1883	Slavey/Hare	Four Gospels
1884	Gwitchin	New Testament
1886	Beaver/Tsattine	Gospel of mark
1887	Muskogee	New Testament
1889	Tsimshian/Sm'algyax	Four Gospels
1891	Haida	Gospel of Matthew
1895	Nisga'a	Gospel of Matthew
1899	Gitxsan	Gospel of Luke
1900	Kwak'wala/Kwakiutl	Four Gospels & Book of Acts
1903	Arapaho	Gospel of Luke
1906	Zuni	Gospel of Mark
1907	Ho-chunk/Winnebago	Four Gospels
1908	Western Cree	Whole Bible
1910	Navajo	Gospel of Mark

1912	Chinook Jargon	Gospel of Mark
1929	Hopi	Four Gospels
1929	Yupik	Psalms & New Testament
1929	Shawnee	The Four Gospels
1933	Keres	Gospel of Matthew
1934	Cheyenne	New Testament
1942	Oneida	Gospel of Luke
1958	Western Apache	Gospel of John
1958	Comanche	Gospel of Mark
1966	Upper Tanana	Gospel of Mark
1968	Kuyukon	Gospel of John
1969	Tewa	Gospel of Mark
1969	Tlingit	Gospel of John
1972	Central Tarahumara	New Testament
1975	Stoney Nakoda	Gospel of Mark
1975	O'odham	New Testament
1977	Northern Paiute	Gospel of Mark

1977	Yaqui	New Testament
1979	Blackfoot/Siksika	Mark and John
1979	Crow/Absaalookah	Gospel of Mark
1980	Mikasukee	Gospel of Mark
1981	Northern Tepehuan	New Testament
1986	Shoshone	Gospel of Mark
1989	Havasupai-Walapai-Yavapai	Gospel of Luke
1993	Algonquin	Gospel of John
1995	Carrier	New Testament
1996	Meskwaki	Gospel of John
2001	Eastern Cree	New Testament
2003	Dogrib	New Testament
2006	Ute/Southern Paiute	Gospel of Luke
2007	Naskapi	New Testament
2007	Chilcotin	Gospel of Mark
2007	Baja Tarahumara	New Testament
2014	Atikamekw	New Testament

This is not a comprehensive list, because all Bible translation is basically work-in-progress. Translation usually starts with some excerpts, then one whole book, then perhaps the four Gospels, and on to a full New Testament. I didn't capture the projects that have not yet matured into at least one full book being translated, and there are many. Also, if a language project had reached a later threshold like Four Gospels or even the full New Testament, then I chose the later date - at which the full bundle was completed. So this could be a bit misleading, because the first book might have been translated several decades earlier.

All I am trying to verify is that – in line with missionary work down through the ages – outreach begins with getting to know a tribe or nation well enough to speak its own language. Then comes the stage of building a vernacular dictionary, followed by translation as outlined above. Then publication and reading of the Bible in the vernacular.

Usually this is followed by literacy training – so members of the tribe can read the Bible for themselves. The roots of this literacy focus are in ancient Israel, which was already a functionally literate nation in 500 BC. That is, *everyone* could read including the women and the staff. Britain was the second country in the world to become functionally literate – in 1898! The United States followed Britain within a few decades. One of the huge gains of the Russian revolution was that in about three decades, it also reached the level of functional literacy. (Bearing in mind, most of the 30 million peasants who starved to death in the meanwhile couldn't read.)

The reason a state wants literacy is different – they want an educated work force which can make the economy boom (so all citizens can fill out their tax returns!). I don't think North America could ever go the way of South Africa, which enshrined nine Bantu languages in its constitution, as well as two European languages. Eleven national languages is complicated – there are not enough sides on a box of cereal to print them all! All the more reason why we should admire and celebrate the missionary endeavor highlighted in the table above to translate scripture into the vernacular. This always has the effect of recording and preserving languages (and thus the culture itself) in a country where English is the one and only official language. "The melting pot."

Going back to 1776, George Washington believed in the assimilation approach, as opposed to extermination. This was somewhat egalitarian. Even the thirteen colonies did not speak one common language. Some spoke English, others German, others Dutch. Not to mention many immigrants. So in the early period before the new capital Washington was built, Congress held a vote on which language should be adopted as the one *lingua franca* of the new nation. English won. By one vote! German almost made it. Here is a reality check: why do missionaries toil away at language study and Bible translation into the vernacular in this context at all? It is because of their respect and love for indigenous people, that's why. This was either in Thomas King's blind spot, or else he didn't want you to know.

On the map it can be noted Pennsylvania is a relatively large state among the thirteen colonies. It was the colony that attracted large numbers of German settlers. It was only exceeded in size by New York. So it was a force – and is still an important state to capture in American elections. When people speak of the "Pennsylvania Dutch", the phrase should really be the Pennsylvania *Deutsch*. This is why German almost won the vote to become the common language.

There is another interesting connection to deep European origins. In 1520, a Czechian landowner was granted the right to mint coins because of a motherlode of silver that he had discovered in his valley. There were only city-states in Europe at the time, so coins were still valued on the basis of their weight. These coins began to circulate widely because of the abundance of silver ore in this mine. By 1530, the town of Joachimsthal near the German border had the biggest mine in Europe and had become the second biggest city in Czechia after Prague. The silver coins came to be known as "thalers" from the name of the town. Without going into too much detail, its use spread to the New World where the name evolved to "dollar". Both the USA and Canada still use "dollar" currencies.

Our currencies evolved from European coins. Our orphanage-technology was imported as well, but it gave way to orphan trains and "placing out" (i.e. fostering and adoption). Our public education system was largely modeled on the social innovations of Bishop Comenius. There is always social innovation and trending going on. "You can't lock up and idea". In the post-Covid world, many families are now abandoning the public education system in favour of homeschooling. A recent study found that significant percentage of learners have not returned to school. Homeschooling saw a 30% increase in 2021-2022 while public school enrollment fell by more than 1.2 million students within the first two years of the COVID-19 pandemic, in the USA.

When people emigrate, they take a lot of things with them - their language, their money, their faith, their customs, their music. There was another huge immigration to the USA – from Africa. By far the highest volume of African slaves imported into the USA was in the century before 1776. Then it tapered off significantly. It didn't stop, but it shrank. It must have been slowly dawning on American leaders, the values and principles espoused in the Bill of Rights had major social implications. Voices in the churches were already speaking out. Or at least consciences. Britain's Anti-Slavery Bill was also arresting the Atlantic Slave Trade. And to be consistent - the evidence is there in the table above, that there were also missionaries who were near and dear to the First Nations throughout. They learned their languages, and preached the Good News to them about the Prince of Peace. In their own language.

There is an interesting trajectory in The Inconvenient Indian. The first four chapters are about the distant past. Then come three chapter (5 -7) about the recent past and the historical present. In chapter 5, Thomas King roars about the residential schools. Then in chapter 6 he covers the twentieth century and in chapter 7, he picks up from 1985 on (the historic present). So the century before 1985 is where the residential schools debacle comes into the narrative. The last three chapters explore the future – where this is going.

In the first four chapters, I find only nine specific references to Christianity, the church or missionaries. Whereas, chapter 5 about the residential schools is peppered with jabs. In chapter 6 about the twentieth century there are only three jabs. In the (post-1985) chapter 6 it is down to only one jab. That leaves chapters 7 – 10, where quite honestly the jabs are few and far between. Only one each in chapters 8 and 9, then chapter 10 is jab-free. This leaves an impression that

Christian mission has been neutralized. It was a player early on, but after the churches apologized for the residential schools (there is a list of apologies on page 132, about half-way through the book), the role of religion fades way.

I think this trajectory is misleading. Twelve of the Bible translations listed in the table above are after 1985. That is 18 percent of the 67 translations done over the past 350 years. I believe Christian outreach still has momentum, and there may already be missionaries from First Nations to other tribes or even to other continents. Just as there are now indigenous people in the parliaments of both the USA and Canada.

And what about revival among the First Nations? Sharon Stands-Over-Bull is both a pastor and Crow elder. In 1906, her grandmother attended the Azusa Street Revival in California. The grandmother returned to her Crow reservation in Montana filled with the Holy Spirit. Her church has gone from strength to strength. Now Sharon's husband Russell is quoted in CBN News on 31 January 2023: "Whole communities were touched by the fire of the Holy Spirit, and the Crows eventually became known throughout Indian Country as the center for Pentecost. This was the capital for Pentecost, and still is considered that by many neighboring tribes."

I don't think anyone who is as well informed as Thomas King doesn't know about this phenomenon. Or the demography... for in the 2011 census in Canada, 63 percent of indigenous people self-identified as Christian, compared to 67 percent on the non-indigenous side. These are very similar readings that make me wonder how many indigenous people concur with the author's critique of Christianity. Of course it varies from one place to another. In Nunavut, 93 percent of people self-identify as Christian. It could vary from those living on reserves, off-setting the majority of indigenous people who now live off-reserve. Revisionists are turning a blind eye to this reality on the ground.

Outreach was never about the race for converts between Catholics and Protestants, as the book alleges on pages 118 and 119. Both do missionary work. I regard this as complementarity not as competition. Conversion to Christianity (of any denomination) does not subdue local culture. Three generations after Asuza street revival, Sharon Stands-Over-Bull is still proudly Crow. However, during an era when the prevalent government policy was assimilation (read: government overreach), the church's historical role in education was captured, causing contortions.

I am not disputing that the residential schools debacle was a fiasco. It was. There is no getting around it. So were the Crusades. So was apartheid, which collapsed soon after it was declared a heresy by the World Council of Churches at its Ottawa conference in 1986. The South Africa Council of Churches had already declared it as a heresy in 1982. But Ronald Reagan and Maggie Thatcher had a way of jointly slowing down the pace of change. (Another example of the distinction between public policy and church advocacy.) After all, the UN General Assembly had already declared apartheid to be a "crime against humanity" in 1966. But apartheid was so inter-twined with the Dutch Reformed church in South Africa, that it took some time and global pressure for it to trickle down from the political level to the deeper spiritual and moral level. Then through repentance by the DRC, triggered by the Kairos Document, it could be dispensed with.

It is possible to express regrets for the residential schools debacle without losing overall esteem and respect for missionaries, the church and Christianity.

When extraordinary wrongdoing is implied, but not proven, truth suffers along with many who may not be culpable, but are included by association. But the suffering does not stop there. It can extend to undoubted victims of the wrongdoing, who are misled. There is of this outcome in some revisionist treatments of the emerging story of "unmarked graves" at many sites of former residential schools.

First in Kamloops, British Columbia and now in other locations, First Nations have reported early results of ground penetrating radar (GPR) surveys at former school sites. To their credit, most chiefs and band leaders have been careful to describe these results as "possible graves", "plausible graves" or by similar qualifiers. As of this writing, none have been excavated to confirm there are graves, and if so, the approximate date of death, the identity of the deceased, including their ages at death, and the cause of death, whether by violence or disease. These further investigations may or may not follow. Much depends on decisions to be taken by First Nations and band leadership, taking into account their cultural concerns, which in some cases may preclude excavation or forensic work, and the wishes of the indigenous people. Decisions on further work may vary from one First Nation or band to another.

Meanwhile, many commentators, both indigenous and non-indigenous, claim these preliminary results confirm a pattern of more than neglect, but of murder, of indigenous children at the hands of residential school personnel, including particularly priests, nuns and other missionary workers.

A long-time, highly qualified elementary public school teacher in Abbotsford, British Columbia was recently fired, for responding to a student who told the class all the unmarked graves were those of children murdered by priests.

The teacher responded to say disease was prevalent in the schools and may have claimed many lives. At first, the teacher was admonished by management. When he claimed his innocence, he was fired.

GPR results are not the only evidence we have of the failure of indigenous residential schools in Canada. There are many stories, some first-hand, some passed down through indigenous generations, of wrongdoing. But there is still a large gap in the available evidence, as indigenous leaders acknowledge. This includes government and church records, which have been very slow to be released. We also know the death rate among indigenous people, and particularly children, from infectious disease, including tuberculosis, was very high in the years when these schools operated – much higher than in the general population. We know this was due to overcrowding, inadequate health care, and likely also a weakness in indigenous immunity to diseases originating in Europe.

All this tells a fair-minded person that it is premature to imply that possible or plausible unmarked graves establish systematic, murderous practice at indigenous residential schools.

Incidentally, drug-resistant TB is currently raging in South Africa. Around 300,000 cases are diagnosed annually. It is highly contagious and HIV prevalence has weakened people's immunity. With almost six million sero-positive citizens, the high rate of TB infection is not surprising. Especially among those who lived in crowded settings with poor ventilation. I have recently lost two good South Africa friends to drug-resistant TB, in as many years. It is a near and present danger.

The wisest chiefs and band leaders are cautious in reporting what they have found and what is yet to be done. They understand the damage that can be done to their own people, many of whom profess the Christian faith, by the spread of claims, which may ultimately not be proven, or proven false in some material respect. Unfortunately, too many others rush to judgement – condemning the Christian institutions involved, and too often, by extension, the whole church and its missionary workers everywhere in all ages. This serves no one – particularly not indigenous people and certainly not Christians and those whom they seek to serve.

Pre-judgment is bias. And bias is discriminatory. It is time to be fair.

Nelson Mandela encountered missionaries throughout his career, from working as a gardener when he was a student to his encounters with the late, great Father Trevor Huddleson – anti-apartheid activist par excellence. In his autobiography, Mandela weighs it up this way. He was writing of mission schools in general, not specifically about the residential schools in North America: "These schools have often been criticized for being colonialist in their attitudes and practices. Yet, even with such attitudes, I believe their advantages outweighed their disadvantages". Have we thrown out the baby with the bathwater?

8. PARADIGMS LOST, AND FOUND

Is apartheid alive and well and living in the Haudenosaunee Confederacy?

According to Thomas King, his book is a work-in-progress. He has been collecting relevant materials for over 50 years. So his book is loaded with interesting and useful facts, figures and stories. The version I read came out in 2017. The first white settlements in America were over 400 years ago. Plus there were several different colonial powers, each with their own language and distinct policies. So there is a lot to keep track of, and it all gets quite heavy and overwhelming at times.

I am going to try to round up what I read. Let's start with the problem analysis. Because if you don't understand a problem, it will be hard to solve. That could explain all the zigs and zags along the trail? I think a line on page 86 gets close to the bone: "the old savagism versus civilization dichotomy". The author regards it as toxic and anti-democratic.

On this – as a veteran missionary – I could not agree more. We speak of cultural relativism versus cultural hegemony. On the one hand, you have Benjamin Franklin inviting the Iroquois Confederacy to attend his 1754 Albany Congress. This was early days but it would seem they were invited *inter pares* (between equals). Whether they were seen as allies or just as noble savages occupying the same space, is not clear to me. At least there was not an air of superiority, which emerged later as America's manifest destiny to deliver liberty, civilization and religion to the rest of the world. But how?

I said I agree with Thomas King on this problem statement. That is because I don't think cultural hegemony is a suitable approach for missiology.

The starting paradigm is **Segregation**. We don't speak one another's languages. We want to meet in various arenas like praying towns, Catholic Indian villages, or trading posts. And as the years turn into decades and European immigration speeds up, not much changes. There is such a disconnect between us, that when the Meech Lake Accord was negotiated in Canada, the First Nations were excluded. Quebec was on track to get "sovereignty", aboriginals were not even at the negotiating table. This is the starting point – two entirely different paradigms occupying the same continent, but worlds apart. There are two road maps out of segregation – extermination or assimilation.

Extermination (or annihilation) had various manifestations – diseases, ambushes, battlefields, and cruel relocations. In the current arena, bigotry and racism take on other manifestations, but they still linger. Perhaps hate-speech or intimidation? The message is simple – we don't want to share the same space with you. Well, this can also get stuck in segregation mode, although the Rwanda genocide in 1994 was a reminder that it can boil over very quickly - as Roméo Dallaire can tell you. He was the Canadian army officer who led the ill-fated UN peacekeeping mission in Kigali. What happened was like a tsunami of racism in which 800 000 lives were lost. There was very little the blue helmets could do, because their warnings had fallen on deaf ears.

Speaking of getting stuck in segregation, in fact that happened a lot. First Nations were ring-fenced into reservations or "Indian land". Worse yet, they were often relocated – like the Trail of Tears. This meant abrogating treaties which had previously been agreed to. Probably the biggest-ever forced-relocation happened in 1948 – in India and Pakistan - where it was called "Partition". By comparison, the unsuccessful relocation of the Mi'kmac in Nova Scotia was tiny. Relocation or "partition" forces people to segregate.

At first, the colonies were on the eastern seaboard – east of the Appalachian Mountains. Then rising population pressure (i.e. demand for land) pushed the "red line" back to the Mississippi River. The Law did not permit whites to buy land from indigenous people, who had always seen the land as communal anyway, belonging to their tribe and not to individuals. So only the tribe could negotiate land deals and only with the federal government, not with the constituent states. So in a way, reservations were sort of mini-states, within bigger states. But both the states and these mini-states were obliged to deal with "the feds".

One form of annihilation is genocide. The existence of treaties – of which there are hundreds - suggests that initial policies favoured segregation. Sharing the same space. But annihilation was obviously on General Sherman's mind when he said that the more Indians he killed this year were the less he would have to kill next year. The question of whether genocide was committed in the residential schools debacle is dealt with in the next chapter.

Assimilation came to be the paradigm of choice, but even this came in many forms. The perennial goal was to absorb indigenous people into the social fabric of America. Now let's get our bearings. America was receiving immigrants from all over the place. They came in through ports like New York and San Francisco. They were obliged to learn English and within a generation or two most of them did. They might still speak their native tongue at home, for a generation or two? But it was a survival imperative to learn English, in this melting pot. Even all the colonists who joined the fight for USA independence couldn't even speak to one another as a number of European languages were spoken, so it was agreed first that a *lingua franca* was needed, and second that it would be English. Those of us who grow up in a unilingual environment may now resist bilingualism or learning many languages. But for missionaries, learning at least one other language is an imperative.

Speaking of fighting alongside people you can't speak to, the First Nations fought on both sides of the war of USA independence and also the War of 1812. Tribes based in Canada fought for the British and those based in the USA took up arms to defend their homeland. Canada has dealt with immigrants somewhat differently, in that they can opt to learn French instead of English, and are encouraged to stay connected to their culture of origin. This has created "cultural enclaves" – like Mennonite colonies where German or Icelandic was spoken. Or like Chinatown. Democracy has conjoined majority-rule with the rights of minorities. Some of the largest Italian and Portuguese communities are now in Canadian cities!

When the tribes of Europe went to war, it always spilled over into the colonies. Later, the USA had to fight the tribes of Europe at times – namely the British and the Spanish. And eventually, the Germans. So you had mega-trends like the Louisiana Purchase whereby America bought out a large French holding in the wild west and expanded towards the Pacific Ocean. Parts of Mexico were also swallowed and each expansion brought with it more indigenous nations, tribes and bands.

But there was something of a double standard in this – assimilating all immigrants while segregating the First Nations. So it is not surprising governments were exploring ways to assimilate indigenous people as well.

In the push towards assimilation, there were three main thrusts as I see it. In the USA, there was "allotment" in 1887; then the residential schools from about that time until late in the 20th century; and finally "termination" in 1953. Similar policies were tried in Canada, as noted on the go.

Allotment was an attempt to get alignment in the USA between "Indian land" and the rest of America. As noted above, the First Nations saw land as communal, not individual. However, everywhere else in America, you could buy or sell parcels of land. So allotment set out to sub-divide reservations into plots – bigger for families and smaller for individuals. While implementing this policy, the feds managed (by sleight of hand) to shrink the overall holdings of the First Nations. This was corrupt, once again basically ignoring the treaties. It was also a kind of colonization-of-the-mind... trying to get indigenous people to think individualistically instead of communally.

The **residential schools** debacle (in both the USA and Canada) was an educational innovation that failed miserably. Originally there had been day schools on the reservations (USA) and reserves (Canada). There were also some boarding schools on reservations and reserves. Then came some integration into non-indigenous schools, not unlike the "busing" that was later used to end the segregation of white and black school children. This was getting to the edge of what has since come to be called "mainstreaming". Sometimes indigenous schools existed off-reservation too. These were all channeled into residential schools.

Starting with the Carlisle school in Pennsylvania, this new model was adopted. Thomas King describes it on page 145: "Children were forcibly removed from their homes and kept at the schools. As with their U.S. counterparts, schools insisted that the children not have any extensive contact with their families or home communities. Students were forbidden

139

to speak their languages or practice any part of their culture."

This was deplorable. It is cultural hegemony. It is bad missiology and totally out of sync with the efforts of missionaries to esteem and respect local culture, to learn the languages, translate the Bible and offer literacy training – the time honored baseline of missionary work. How could missionaries busy themselves with Bible translation and literacy and then tell school children not to speak in their own language? No one can explain that discrepancy to me.

Jesus started a movement that came to be known in the Roman Empire as "the Third Way". The first way was Rome's way – wielding military power and dispensing justice. The second way was Jewish business and commerce. Everywhere you went in the empire, the Jews were the merchants and entrepreneurs. The third way taught love and forgiving. The way of the cross.

Is there any way to harmonize the history of missions with the residential schools debacle? The answer may come from Ward Churchill on page 131 of The Inconvenient Indian: "the schools were national policy". (Ward Churchill wrote a book about the residential schools, published in 2004 called Kill the Indian, Save the Man.)

Thomas King cites two government studies of the residential schools, neither of which were favourable. First, a 1928 study in the USA by Lewis Merian, co-authored by a colleague from the Winnebago tribe of Nebraska. Second, a 1966 study in Canada called "the Hawthorne Report". Both were fundamentally against segregation. They would both be more in favour of mainstreaming, although that word had not been coined yet. Also it sounds a bit like an exit strategy to leave the reservations. How on earth did they think that by ring-fencing them into these isolated institutions that they were promoting assimilation? It boggles the mind.

Like Allotment, this strategy of residential schools crashed. People are still picking up the pieces, as this reaches up to living memory. One take-away in my view is that even though this model of education failed miserably, it does not negate the advantage of having an education. After all, education-for-all is a global campaign. Sustainable Development Goal number four is "quality education".

Going back to evolving orphan technology. At one stage when new orphanages were built, they intentionally raised the windows quite high off the floor. This let the light in, but kept the children from seeing the real world outside. This was unethical, as it alienated orphans as opposed to integrating them. Some African languages have no word for "orphan", because these minors have always been absorbed into other families. Orphanages served a purpose, but we are glad better solutions have been found. Back to the future with adoption.

Another take-away is that despite the bitterness of this failed residential school model, I do not agree there is any problem with education anchored in Christianity. I see that as a revisionist bias. This debacle might never have happened where parents could determine which school they wanted their children to attend. If they want them in a Christian school or a madrasse, then so be it. Probably some unsuspecting families did want their children to attend church schools. It does not sound like missionary methodology that children could not ever speak in their own tongue. Certainly one good way to learn a language is "immersion". The schools would have emptied if families could have voluntarily pulled their kids out of a school they didn't like. The doctrine of separation of church and state in the USA means that churches are private, voluntary organizations (PVOs). They do not have the authority to forcibly remove children from their homes and intern them at a school. But the negative impact of this failure has caused the pendulum to swing to where state overreach is now leading us past "freedom of worship" to "freedom from worship".

I suspect the sheer size of government grew exponentially over the period of the residential schools debacle. Mission schools and hospitals were being absorbed into public education and health care. This was especially true during the Great Depression years when PVOs could not keep pace with the demand for social assistance. Residential schools existed for indigenous children only, but they were still under federal government policy. Between this dominance of public policy and the concurrent rise of evolutionary humanism, the children in residential schools were caught in a tragic pincer effect.

Many years later, Ronald Reagan would say the nine most dangerous words in English are: "I'm from the government and I'm here to help." If we fatalistically accept government overreach with a shrug, we will become a nanny state. Civil liberties are there for a reason.

Then came **Termination** in 1953 in the USA. It has a nasty ring to it, like the Terminator. But it was new legislation aimed at giving a new impetus to assimilation. Once again it meant abrogating treaties, but this time – all treaties. The plan was to abolish all federal supervision of indigenous tribes. This would basically force First Nations to assimilate.

This policy only lasted for thirteen years in the USA. Then termination was terminated! In the meanwhile, 109 tribes had been officially terminated and a million acres of "Indian land" lost. Canadian PM Pierre Trudeau, generally regarded as a "progressive", made an unsuccessful attempt to introduce termination in Canada in 1969.

As a Canadian missionary of Irish descent, I have spent over half my life in Africa. I would like to share some African perspectives, as I spent many years of my life as an anti-apartheid activist. I made a huge emotional investment in fighting apartheid. So I was a bit taken aback when I read (on pages 206 and 207 of The Inconvenient Indian) about the trip that the Iroquois Nationals lacrosse team attempted to the International Lacrosse Championships in Manchester, England, in 2010. They travelled on Haudenosaunee passports. The Canadian contingent entered the USA on a special one-time waiver that they obtained with the help of Senator Hilary Clinton. They left New York for England, and guess what? They were refused entry into England.

This is greatly symbolic. Basically, the sovereignty claimed by the Mohawks, the Navajo and the Blackfoot – all of which issue passports to travelling tribe members – makes them akin to Bantustans. These South African "homelands" used to issue their own passports too. Of course South African blacks were also required to carry "pass books" when

144

circulating outside their homeland inside South Africa. Much of the bitterness generated by apartheid centred on these pass laws. They were totally discriminatory. On page 211 of the book, Harald Cardinal is quoted – author of <u>The Unjust Society</u>: "We do not want the Indian Act retained because it is a good piece of legislation. It isn't. It is discriminatory from start to finish... but we would rather continue to live in bondage under the inequitable Indian Act than surrender our sacred rights." This is the dilemma facing the First Nations in the future. The debate continues...

The opposite point of view is "neo-termination". In other words, to reach rapprochement between indigenous and non-indigenous, all treaties and tribes should be scrapped altogether.

At the beginning of Grand Apartheid, brought to you by the Boers starting in 1948, there was a lot of talk of "the right to self-determination" and the importance of mutual respect between distinct cultures. This had actually begun already under the British with the Native Land Act in 1913. The Boers just refined it and took it to scale. To the blacks, it entrenched dispossession of their land – for they were sequestered or ring-fenced into specified areas. It was segregation. The British identified distinct Bantu tribes, along the north and eastern borders, and created enclaves for them. When the Boers won the 1948 election, overtaking 150 years of British policy predominance, these were upgraded (or should I say downgraded?) into Bantustans. This was identity politics at its worst, and the world is not going to go along with a re-run of apartheid now in North America. Trending is going in the opposite direction.

The British were big on segregation. As illustrated in their "partition" of India and Pakistan in 1948. In their view, this meant both cultures (in South Africa there were several on both sides) had value, so each needed its own space. Proportional to its population and economic ambitions. This is not unlike the concept of reserves in Canada and reservations in the USA.

But my Mozambican friends have explained this to me in a different way. For the official Portuguese policy was always assimilation. They had no problem with inter-racial marriage (which was illegal under Grand Apartheid in South Africa). Blacks could even get Portuguese citizenship, but the proviso was they must learn to speak Portuguese, get an education and convert to Catholicism. They could indeed become part of the government and military establishment, without any hesitation based on race. They became citizens of Portugal and could freely travel to other lusophone ports of call. Remember that Portugal called their colonies "overseas provinces". It was just playing with semantics.

But my Mozambican friends make a distinction – between the "open racism" of South Africa (both Dutch and British) and the "closed racism" of Mozambique and Angola. Their perspective on assimilation is different – *the Portuguese saw zero value in local culture.* The only way forward for blacks was to abandon their respective African culture and religion, and exchange it for Portuguese language, culture and Catholicism.

It seems to me the future of indigenous affairs in North America lies somewhere between the paradigms of segregation and assimilation.

When Mozambique won its independence in 1974, the new regime was Communist, and therefore highly centralized. Sadly, it opted to abandon all tribal structures, although they still remain there informally. One of my best friends is from the royal family of a tribe in Mozambique. He might have become a chief but there are no longer any chiefs. This almost sounds to me like cultural extermination. Although the local languages persist. But slowly, black children in the cities are growing up speaking only Portuguese. To offset this attrition creeping in, there is an effort to create cultural mechanisms to teach tribal lore and customs to future African generations. Even the school curricula need to be revised. One thing that can help is capturing vernacular languages in dictionaries and Bible translations. This is more than an anthropological or linguistic exercise – it is one way for Christians to be "the salt of the earth".

The trending in southern Africa at this time is to try to offer at least foundation education (i.e. Grades 1 and 2) in the vernacular. For children actually learn the content better when they can internalize it in their own tongue.

Whereas in the new and democratic South Africa – starting in 1994 – an effort was made to preserve tribal structures and chiefs. Some of these are controversial like the Ingonyama Trust in KwaZulu-Natal province. It owns thirty percent of the land in that province. This land is basically rented to Zulus by their king. Some see this as a way of making a traditional nation sustainable and others see it as un-democratic regress. It is very controversial.

In my province of Mpumalanga, we have a number of Tribal Authorities. They are ruled by traditional chiefs, although they look much like the peri-urban "townships" near to our towns and cities. I like the term "high-density area" better than "township" but they are not so different from the "bairros" of lusophone Africa or the "favelas" of Brazil. Slums is not a nice word. Remember "Soweto" stands for "South West Townships". These were originally ring-fenced on the south-west side of Johannesburg with only one main highway linking them to the city - so they could be quickly blockaded. Of course blacks took pride in their own neighbourhood and the word Soweto has ironically become famous.

It is sad to recall that at one stage Sowetans had to be out of Joburg by the end of the day, and when they were at work in the city or commuting, they could be stopped by the police and asked for their passbooks. This was the horrible reality of Grand Apartheid. When you stopped at a gas station, there were not two bathrooms but four (two for each gender – black and white).

Today's Tribal Authorities seem to me to work well. Government sets up good infrastructure for the chief and his "indunas". They form a Tribal Council that meets regularly to provide local governance. A permanent staff works at the Tribal Authority offices. If you have a domestic or community problem, you come in the morning and sit under a designated tree waiting to meet the staff. If they cannot resolve your issue, it is put on the agenda of the next Tribal Council meeting. So there is a high degree of devolution or self-determination. You don't have to take matters to court, you can take them to Tribal Council. Above all, these affairs are conducted in the vernacular, and near to where so many people live.

Come to think of it, there is a Department (i.e. Ministry) of Traditional Affairs under a Minister in the Cabinet (the TA in COGTA), to address relevant issues. And a National House of Traditional Leaders that is distilled from provincial houses of traditional leaders. So there is some direct engagement with government decision-making. South Africa does not have a Senate – but it does have a second house in parliament, aside from the National Assembly. That is the National Council of Provinces, which has a unique role – to seek coherence and minimize duplication in the roles of the three tiers of government. I would like to think this vetting includes the Tribal Authorities?

I would steer clear of "neo-termination". But I agree with British Immigration's decision to refuse entry to Mohawks traveling on Haudenosaunee Confederacy passports. That is out-of sync with the prevailing protocols.

There must be a *via media* between segregation and assimilation, to be fair.

9. RE-INVENTING THE MISSIONARY

Do unto others as you would have them do unto you

My vocation is dynamic. It is not static, although it still conserves some core elements. Today there are missionary pilots, for example. Keeping up with technology, Bible translation uses computer tools. So in many ways, building dictionaries of unwritten languages and the translation that follows is sped up. Counseling has now become a major ministry in the church. Perhaps it was always there? But with the rise of psychology as a science, the church has kept apace.

Mission organizations proliferated over the past century. Many church denominations instituted their own outreach arms. Some of these became "NGOs" in their own right. Alternatively, some pastors like Bob Pierce launched "para-church organizations" with independent, coopted Boards. They took relief and development outreach to scale. On the west coast, Bob Pierce founded World Vision which now employs ten thousand people world-wide. He later founded Samaritan's Purse on the east coast, with Franklin Graham now at its helm. Franklin is one of Billy Graham's sons. He is also an evangelist like his father.

Billy Graham took evangelization to scale. His first Los Angeles Crusade in the early 1950s shook that city to its foundations. I could go on and on into Christian radio stations, ships that dock in ports with a hospital on board, and film versions of Gospel stories like The Chosen. Or even more recently, the movie Jesus Revolution.

As I have pointed out in previous chapters, advocating for justice and peace has always been a part of Christian outreach. This is more formal in the tall hierarchy of the Roman Catholic church. For in almost every country, it has a department called the Catholic Commission for Justice and Peace. In South Africa, it was a Dominican priest, Father Stanislaus Muyebe, who first filed a complaint with the Public Protector about "state capture". This has led to major upheavals as the nation tries to treat this cancer of corruption. Someone described to me the difference between a war and a world war. One is between two countries, fighting on a relatively limited scale about a border dispute, but the other is when each and every country's economy is re-tooled to support a massive war effort. That is like the difference between corruption and state capture. Corruption is criminal, but state capture is massively diabolical. The whole national economy is captured by a dictator or cabal, rendering it green pasture for looting and plunder.

Fighting infanticide, suttee, foot-binding, slavery, civil rights and apartheid has moved on - into corruption-busting. In the country where I currently serve as a missionary, civil society and opposition parties have closed ranks to "Save South Africa". This was the name of a loosely-structured coalition to fight state capture. This led to the appointment of a Judicial Inquiry and a damning report from the Zondo Commission. As a result, the ex-liberation movement now in government has been split into two factions. The really hard hitting in South Africa is not between the ruling party and the opposition parties, it is between the two factions of the ANC. And as the African proverb says, "When two elephants are fighting, it is the grass that suffers."

The wages of corruption are unemployment, inequality and poverty. Thus Christian ministry itself has evolved. This is not unlike the current situation of the First Nations in North America, just on a much grander scale. For the official unemployment rate in South Africa is 53 percent. The unofficial rate is probably higher. And as jobs tend to be in the hands of older, more experienced workers, younger citizens – more especially women – face much higher unemployment rates. Of course this feeds the abuse of drugs, which fuels crime, in a downward spiral. The indigenous people of North America face similar challenges. One possible reason that over half of them live off-reservation is they choose to live where conditions are less of a challenge?

This may explain why indigenous people are "overrepresented" in categories associated with social failure. For example, the greatly disproportionate rate of addiction and incarceration, at least in Canada. Fact is, 25 percent of indigenous people in Canada suffer from addiction, compared to 17 percent of the general population. Indigenous people make up 5 percent of the country's population, but 32 percent of its prison population. This is indicative of the underlying problems facing them, which lead to arrest, conviction and prison. The "disease" is not the rate of incarceration, that's just a symptom. Another indicator is the suicide rate, which is six times higher among indigenous youth than their peers in non-Indigenous Canadian populations.

All these new problems are leading to new solutions, new mission methodologies. Winds of change are blowing again. We march, we protest, we investigate, we expose, we blow the whistle, we write, we lay charges, we pursue, we persist, and we litigate. In the next chapter, this inconvenient missionary will enter a mine-field about genocide. Because as a vocation, we have a perennial role in public engagement. This is not about crushing cultures. We still believe in personal renewal; but we believe in social renewal as well.

Bi-culturalism

I said in the last chapter, there are only two roads out of segregation – annihilation or assimilation. That is, if segregation must go. It has occurred to me there is a third alternative to either/or - and that is both/and. Some people do not mind wearing two hats. Here is an example from a friend of mine who is a professor of education:

"In the 1990s, a professor that I know had a colleague at Wits University in South Africa. She was from the BaPedi tribe in Sekhukhune, North East of Pretoria. She had a PhD in Education from Cambridge University and was a brilliant lecturer. One day I asked her, "Do you ever go home to see Agogo?" She said: "Of course, I go home to my village every three months. I take off my Western clothes, kick off my shoes, put on an African dress and sit on the dirt floor and talk with the other women for three days. I do this because that is who I am!""

"This lady was in charge of training for the whole of the South African Public Service. She did an incredibly good job, but that is not who she is! This begs the question, why should a highly intelligent person like her have to spend most of her time being something she would prefer not to be, just to put bread on the table? In South Africa, the Afrikaners behave as Afrikaners, and the people with an English and

Portuguese background do the same. It is only the Africans that have to be two persons in one – and it is their country!"

This is a strategy. And it is a way of life that is not unfamiliar to missionaries. They serve in a foreign context, and are not always "peregrini". They may serve for two years or two decades, but they must return to their "home". But reverse culture shock upon reentry can be a bit unsettling. It can lead to identity crisis. Here is an observation by a Catholic priest named Henri Nouwen, from his book Creative Ministry (page 83, 84): "When, however, we find people who have truly devoted themselves to work in the slums and the ghettos and who feel that their vocation is to be of service there, we find that they have discovered that in the smiles of the children, the hospitality of the people, the expressions they use, the stories they tell, the wisdom they show, the good they share, there is hidden so much richness and beauty, so much affection and human warmth, that the work they are doing is only a small return for what they have already received. In this respect we can better understand those many missionaries who, after living for years in the poorest circumstances, nonetheless became homesick for their missions as soon as they returned to their affluent country. It was not because they wanted to suffer more, but because they had found a beauty in their people which they missed in their home community...."

"...when we start discovering that in many ways we are the poor and those who need our help are the wealthy, who have a lot to give, no true social agent gives in to the temptation of power since he has discovered that his task is not a heavy burden or a brave sacrifice but an opportunity to see more and more of the face of Him whom he wants to meet. I wish that more books were written about the so-called "poor" countries and "poor" cities, not only to show how poor they are and how much help they need, but also to show the beauty of their lives, their sayings, their customs, their way of life. Perhaps a new form of Christian "tourism" could then develop in which those who travel can enrich their lives with the wisdom, knowledge and experience of their hosts."

Missionary motives exclude getting rich. According to CNBC, which in early 2023 scoped the ten worst-paying college majors, five years after graduation - the lowest-paid major is theology. I second the emotion. Being a missionary involves a lifetime of sacrifice. We have to live the Stockdale paradox, finding a *via media* between la-la land romanticism and fiscal realism that can quickly sink you into depression. We are very wide awake and not lost in denialism.

Tribalism

I have spent six years of my missionary career living in Zimbabwe. I was there during the 1980s when the *Gukurahundi* took place. Twenty thousand Ndebeles were exterminated by Robert Mugabe's fifth brigade. Thousands were tortured and 400,000 citizens were brought to the brink of starvation - for political motives. This is usually called a genocide, although both the Shona and the Ndebele are Bantu tribes. So it was not racism, but it was certainly tribalism. The then-director of the Catholic Commission of Justice and Peace was a friend of mine. He was constantly in and out of jail for his advocacy efforts. I admired him so much.

In the 21st century, we live in a time when tribalism is in aggressive revival. Everyone feels a need to belong to a "values tribe", be it defined by race, ethnicity, faith, colour, sex, sexual orientation, or some other characteristic. People who cannot find a tribe (usually white folks) *"self-identify"*. Some even *"self-identify"* as indigenous, which has become a problem in Canada, particularly in universities, where fakes have been uncovered. The syllabus for the Law Society of BC's course on indigenous culture contains a forward by Marie Turpel Lafonde, a noted indigenous leader, former judge and professor. Except, CBC recently revealed she is not indigenous. She has been wearing a mask. This came out after the syllabus was published. This was more than identity theft of an individual. *Self-identifying* is one thing, identity fraud is quite another.

I can't remember a time in my life when people everywhere were so divided. This division leads very naturally to a sense of "*victimhood*". The tribe has been victimized, so, I am a victim. Of course, victimhood has no meaning whatsoever unless the perpetrator can be identified. Every victim, to be a victim, must have a perpetrator. The most convenient perpetrator is, of course, the state. After that, it is a small step to the church, which is often identified as mostly white. Another fallacy.

Prime Minister Justin Trudeau likes to say he promotes "diversity and inclusion". These two words are constantly on his lips. He just stands for them. (Diversity of thought does not seem to be included in his definition of that word.) Many other leaders in politics and other sectors follow suit. I'll tell you what it means...

"Diversity" is not a philosophy. It's a fact. It either exists or it does not. In Canada, due to our history and continuing immigration from all over the world, it exists. Multiculturalism was one of Pierre Trudeau's favorite topics. It was and is the Canadian way, as opposed the melting pot in the USA. So, on that point, his son Justin states the obvious.

"Inclusion" is never defined. But it is not very far removed from "assimilation", at least to some degree. Not the same, but it can lead there. When you try to include diverse folk in your business, your school, your club, your church, your community – and you should – over time some degree of assimilation is inevitable. That's what comes of people of different cultures living, working, playing or loving together.

This is not a one way street. Some of the immigrants will be assimilated into the whole, of which we all are now a part, bringing with them elements of their own culture. The evil in tribalism comes in compulsion. Assimilation, like diversity, is just a fact of nature. Not to be feared or loathed – unless you are tribal and nothing else...

Let's consider for a moment the Rwanda genocide in 1994. It was the same year of the first-ever free and democratic elections in South Africa. This was the end of apartheid, when Nelson Mandela was elected. Simultaneously, 800,000 Tutsis were annihilated by their Hutu neighbours. The high moral ground that Africa gained by finding a way past apartheid without civil war was diminished by the horrors in Rwanda the very same year.

Then in 2001, South Africa hosted the UN World Conference on Racism, Racial Discrimination, Xenophobia and Related Intolerance. The charter that emerged in Durban was supposed to be grounded in the success of defeating apartheid. But the whole conference was held under the shadow of the recent Rwanda genocide. The four topics of the conference named above are attitudes, not actions. But they give rise to actions like hate-speech, xenophobia riots, tribal warfare and genocide.

One question is whether the Rwanda genocide was an outbreak of racism or tribalism? Fact is, the Hutus are Bantus and the Tutsi are Nilotics. These are two races. The genocide was implementable because it was and is so easy to tell them apart. Unlike the Arians and the Semitics, who were mixed into the population of Germany, and not easy to tell apart. But they were two white races, thus the Holocaust was racist. It was based on the assumption that the Arian race was superior. Likewise, the Rwanda genocide was an action generated by racist attitudes. Perhaps best captured by the use of the term "cockroaches" to describe the Tutsis by the instigators of the genocide.

I first read <u>Anti-Semite and Jew</u> in a philosophy course as an undergraduate student. Its author Jean Paul Sartre was one of the existentialist philosophers, and he familiarized me with this topic. I went on to become an anti-apartheid

161

activist, because the focus of the struggle against racism shifted from the Jews of Germany to the blacks of South Africa in the 1950s. I started university in the 1960s and later joined the ranks of anti-apartheid activists. Then I became a missionary in one of the "front-line states" – Angola. It was at war with the "racist regime" of South Africa when I arrived to serve as a rural development officer for a national church denomination. I worked for a "mission-planted church" as opposed to one of the independent AICs (African initiated churches).

I drilled wells in villages, installing handpumps so that Angolans could drink potable water. I lived in a home that was built almost a century earlier by a Swiss missionary who was something of a "slavery observatory". This was long after the Atlantic Slave Trade had ended, but Angola was still being raided by the Portuguese for slaves to take to São Tomé, an island not far off the coast. São Tomé produced cacao and coffee and one of its biggest export customers was the Cadbury chocolate firm. The Cadburys were a Christian family from Britain and they got wind of this chicanery – from missionaries serving in Angola. Cadbury threatened to boycott São Tomé in 1898, and that finally brought it to an end.

Although the practice of "forced labour" continued in lusophone Africa, just as slavery in the USA was followed by a long period of "convict leasing". This was a system in which southern states leased prisoners to private railways, mines, and large plantations. While the states profited, prisoners earned no pay and faced inhumane, dangerous, and often deadly work conditions. Similarly, Angolans and Mozambicans were conscripted to work up to six months a year for the business concessions operating in what was then called Portuguese West Africa and Portuguese East Africa respectively.

I was privileged to get to know Rev José Chipenda, who had spent time in Geneva at the World Council of Churches, as a spokesman for the struggle against racism. By his time in that role, the focus had swung from the Holocaust to apartheid.

The Durban Declaration of the World Conference on Racism, Racial Discrimination, Xenophobia and Related Intolerance sounds a warning. It speaks in the Preamble of being: "*Alarmed* by the emergence and continued occurrence of racism, racial discrimination, xenophobia and related intolerance in their more subtle and contemporary forms and manifestations."

Then in clause 17: "We note the importance of paying special attention to new manifestations of racism, racial discrimination, xenophobia and related intolerance to which youth and other vulnerable groups might be exposed."

New manifestations of racism will continue to emerge in future. They have to be identified and confronted. Twenty years on, a follow-up conference was held, also in Durban. Twelve countries pulled out of the 2021 conference: France, Israel, the USA, Canada, Australia, Germany, the UK, Hungary, Austria, Netherlands, the Czechia and Bulgaria.

It is hard to imagine a meaningful conference on racism without the presence of Israel and Germany, for the focus of this topic for much of the past century was the Holocaust. Without the USA, France, the UK, Australia and Canada, the conference was doomed – not to failure, but to be pro-racism instead of anti-racism.

The centerpiece of this boycott was South Africa's pronouncements about the State of Israel and its Palestinian policies. This is frequently called "apartheid" in South Africa. To many listeners, it sounded too much like anti-Semitism. For example, here is a tweet from one Foreign Ministry: (Bulgaria) "will not participate in the UNGA high-level meeting on the Durban Declaration & Plan of Action. Given the history of the process, there's a risk that the forum could be misused for anti-Semitic propaganda. We stay committed to fighting racism in all its forms and manifestations."

Certainly racism can lead to new manifestations, as well as to old ones like genocide. But were the Abraham Accords that far off the mark?

Curiously, another controversial cause in the media these days is indigenous children being adopted by "white Christians". Some would say that this is just another step towards assimilation. But others take exception, accusing the families adopting indigenous children of racism. Is this a new manifestation of racism? There have been surges of inter-racial adoption like the Korean orphans in the 1950s. Was that racism? When a white family adopts a black child, are they guilty of evolutionary humanism, a sense of superiority? Or is it Christian love and care?

The "chilling effect"; burning down churches; public humiliation by tearing down statues of its heroes; imprisoning its prophets; banning prayer in public; firing people for unpopular takes when there is room for doubt - these actions are all new and nasty manifestations of discrimination.

It is always wise to be fair.

10. GENOCIDE & CULTURAL GENOCIDE

This word has an interesting history. It was coined by a Polish Jew, Raphael Lemkin in 1944. It was likely coined from the Greek, "*genos*", meaning birth, genus or kind, and the Latin "*cide*", meaning cut or kill. So, the standard is high for any policy or action to meet the definition. It is one of those words with both an "ordinary" (i.e., dictionary) meaning and a legal meaning, often in the realm of criminal law. They are similar, but not identical. Like all such words, the use of the term "genocide", without qualification or any indication of the sense in which the word is used, can lead to misunderstanding.

The typical dictionary definition is "the deliberate killing of a large number of people from a particular nation or ethnic group with the aim of destroying that nation or group" (Oxford). The word "deliberate" conveys "*intent*", in this case, to kill. The words "with the aim ..." go to motive. Intent and motive are not the same thing. Intent in this context means the perpetrator meant to do what he did, kill – requiring the mental capacity to form that intent. Purpose goes to the perpetrator's aim – why he did what he did. What did he want to achieve?

So, in considering whether the dictionary definition is met, motive is essential. A mere slaughter not directed at destruction of an identifiable nation or group is terrible, but it's not genocide. It is entirely fair, in the context of the dictionary definition, to seek evidence of motive, and not to assume it.

There are other definitions, including those with legal consequences. The most important of these is likely that contained in the UN Convention on the Prevention of the Crime of Genocide, adopted in 1948. It reads:

"In the present Convention, genocide means any of the following acts committed with **intent to destroy,** in whole or in part, a national, ethnical, racial or religious group, as such:

(a) Killing members of the group;

(b) Causing serious bodily or mental harm to members of the group;

(c) Deliberately inflicting on the group conditions of life calculated to bring about its physical destruction in whole or in part;

(d) Imposing measures intended to prevent births within the group;

(e) Forcibly transferring children of the group to another group."

In the Convention definition, subparagraphs (a) to (e) describe the acts – the what – of the offense. To meet the definition, the perpetrator must form the intent to carry out one of these enumerated acts, having the mental capacity to do so. The phrase "intent to destroy ... a group" is used to describe the purpose or aim of the perpetrator – the why.

It is easy to see the Convention definition - a legal definition applicable to the Convention - is broader than the typical dictionary definition. It includes, in addition to killing, other events. Among them are forcible transfer of children to another group. In the case of residential schools, there will be some question as to whether the transfer of indigenous children to a residential school for indigenous children meets the test in subparagraph (e), which refers to *"another group"*. What was the "other group" to which indigenous children were transferred? Nice question, for which I have no answer.

Regardless of whether subparagraph (e) captures the Canadian residential schools experience, the important point here is that all subparagraphs (a) through (e) do not stand alone. Any accurate grammatical interpretation tells us the act must be taken "with the intent to destroy... a group". So, unlike most other crimes, genocide requires proof of motive, not just the intent to commit a deliberate act – e.g. transferring children. The aim is crucial to the crime of genocide, and it is very fair to question whether the evidence establishes motive. This is just and fair, because genocide is one of the most vile - we might say the most vile - of crimes. It should not be alleged without compelling evidence of motive.

In the case of the Holocaust, by way of example, the evidence of motive – the extermination of the Jews – was overwhelming in both documentary and oral testimony at Nuremburg. There was no question.

I must confess that I agree, at times it was hard to tell the difference between assimilation and extermination. This suggests that evidence of extermination – i.e. destruction of the group – is, at the least, unclear. That is not compelling proof of an aim to destroy. It's compelling proof of doubt, and nothing more. The intent of the policy was not to destroy, it was to assimilate.

I hear the echo of my Mozambican friends saying the assimilation policy of the Portuguese was "closed racism". The corollary of it was indigenous cultures were of no value at all. That is not multiculturalism.

169

Cultural Genocide

It is told that a Scottish evangelist and a white father turned up in the court of the Mutessa of the Buganda on the same day. They amused the Mutessa by arguing in his presence for some time before he dismissed them. The Madi and the Mutessa met one day and the Mutessa shared about the time he spent with the missionaries. The Madi told him: "Be careful of these people. They will be nice to you for a while and then they will insist you put away all your wives but one. And if you do not do it, their armies will arrive and force you to do it!"

The Truth and Reconciliation Commission found, in its final report in 2015, the Canadian residential schools system constituted "cultural genocide". This is the TRC's term and is not a legal finding of genocide or even a statement that the dictionary definition, unqualified by "cultural" was met.

Shortly thereafter, the then Chief Justice of Canada, Beverly Mclaughlin, stated publicly the same thing – the system was "cultural genocide". This was as public statement by the Chief Justice, not in a court judgment. Her comment was not a legal conclusion.

For several years, commentators and the media used the phrase "cultural genocide". But increasingly, the qualifier was dropped. Government, and its implementers of policy, including the church, are now accused simply of "genocide". This reflected not so much new, compelling evidence, as increasing hyperbola. The discovery of "possible or plausible graves" certainly played a part, despite the preliminary nature of that evidence as to whether the anomalies were bodies, and if so, who they were, how they died, whether by disease or violence, and who was responsible and why they did what they did, or purpose. So, now most talk is of simply "genocide". This tells us something about the propensity for a rush to judgment where indigenous issues are concerned.

Recently, a Canadian indigenous MP from the New Democratic Party (on the political left) introduced a motion in the House of Commons declaring the residential schools program a "genocide". The motion passed, but that is an opinion of the House that day, and not binding on anyone. The same MP has since called for an amendment of the Criminal Code to provide that "denying that the residential schools program was a genocide" (i.e. denialism) is a crime. The Liberal government minister responsible for indigenous matters said he would consider bringing it forward. It is now very common for media and others to simply declare the residential schools a "genocide".

Using the international or any other criminal law to silence questioning is reprehensible. Is that not criminalizing free speech? Surely we live in an age dominated by propaganda.

When did free speech become right-wing? That was an odd switcheroo, because leftists used to claim intellectual honesty. Democracy was supposedly an "open society" as opposed to the propaganda of despots. The corollary to his question is, since when did you have to be a left-wing to believe in the indigenous peoples' right to self-determination?

Compromising the meaning of "genocide", whether by assuming facts or qualifying the word (i.e. cultural) diminishes the Holocaust, and those who were its victims – six million Jewish men, women and children. The same can be said of the Armenian genocide before, during and after World War I when a million lives were lost in Turkey, Armenia and Syria and the Rwandan genocide in 1994? All these involved deliberate murders, with the aim of annihilation of an identifiable group not neglect or misguided, even cruel policy. Genocide is not a word to be used lightly.

A close look at this definition gets ex-President Thabo Mbeki off the hook for the 350,000 lives lost prematurely to AIDS, because he and his health minister blocked the roll out of anti-retroviral drugs. Many voices are saying that he should be charged with crimes against humanity at The Hague. But it would not lead to a conviction for genocide. Christian voices joined the chorus trying to convince this leader to abide by the prevailing UN conventions. Canada's Stephen

Lewis was Kofi Annan's special advisor on HIV and AIDS. In a meeting with President Thabo Mbeki, Lewis recalls that they almost came to blows because of Mbeki's intransigence, and Lewis' passion for justice. Two card-carrying socialists disagreeing vehemently, when the stakes could not have been much higher.

This is not to say the residential schools policy was good, or not bad or anything. It is accurate to say the policy had serious adverse consequences, some of which echo today. But if that were genocide, all governments in all places at all times would be genocidal. Out of respect to unquestioned victims of genocide, we should not degrade the meaning of the word. We need a word for the Holocaust and the genocides we can prove. Let's protect the veracity of the word "genocide", and the lives of those we know have suffered it.

Can we confidently say today a genocide occurred in the residential schools? Does it meet either the ordinary meaning of the word (dictionary) or the UN definition? Someday, it might. But have we mustered proof? The question of the significance of possible unmarked graves is a very important one. But the evidence to form a reasoned opinion does not exist – yet.

The TRC was commissioned to find the facts. But the commissioners selected were publicly sympathetic to the view that ultimately prevailed. Evidence was extensive, but not under oath and there was no cross-examination, which need not be cruel, but is a key element in truth-finding under our judicial system. Some of the evidence was "hearsay", that is - what one generation had been told by a previous generation. "Hearsay" is useful, but obviously less reliable than direct evidence from a witness who saw the event. There was some contemporary written evidence (e.g. reports), but much of the evidence was oral, which can be less reliable. The government and the religious organizations involved can be faulted for failing to release relevant records, and efforts are still being made to obtain them. There was comparatively little evidence from non-indigenous players. Finally, the TRC report and recommendations were largely simply accepted as truth, with almost no debate. As the years have passed, it has become even more difficult to question the report. There is little interest in dialogue, gaining perspective or hearing and assessing a conflicting, or more fulsome story of the past.

This could explain why the TRC, which included two indigenous judges among the three commissioners, was very careful to qualify their finding, and claim "cultural genocide", a term echoed by the Chief Justice. They may have known the likely motive of most of those who gave their lives to teaching indigenous children was to equip those children to survive in a developed society, which was fast overtaking them on the North American continent and threatened to leave them behind. This effort, which included suppression of indigenous languages and cultural practices, unquestionably and seriously impaired indigenous culture. "Cultural genocide" may not be too strong to describe what was done. Then again in "borrowing" the word genocide, we may be diminishing its true meaning. The church did not seek to kill indigenous people or bring about their "destruction". You might say they sought their survival in a world that was overwhelming them. This could also explain why Pope Francis offered his regrets, but not an apology.

What about character assassination?

The residential schools program has ended up in the scrapyard of social innovations. Perhaps in the shift to assimilation, not all of the sentiments of annihilation were extinguished? Thomas King even suggests that it was hard to tell assimilation and extermination apart, at times. One way or the other, indigenous culture was being marginalized, side-lined and suppressed. But it has recovered and re-rooted to a remarkable extent. It has proven resilient, and is growing. Had federal policy been different – for example just to leave indigenous people alone, avoiding all assimilation efforts - I am not sure we would have seen the same strong resurgence of indigenous cultures we see today. Sometimes, suppression of a culture, while cruel, is the impetus for it to rebound and flourish. The early church comes to mind.

To be fair, I think the residential schools debacle had significant negative impacts. I'm not sure what the alternative might have been in the mid-19th century, when the conditions of that time are taken into account. Thomas King's book tracks the evolving policies in both the USA and Canada which gave rise to this educational innovation. But the 19th century was deeply different from the 21st century. The choices available to us may not have been there at that time. Remember, income tax did not arrive until 1914 in Canada. The role and resources of government were very much constrained, by comparison to our times. Big government tentacles in virtually all cultural activities, including education, as we know them today, still lay in the future. The late 19th century was awash in evolutionary humanism.

The policy of residential schools was conceived by government (in both the USA and Canada), which was taking over the role of educating citizens. Perhaps unwisely, the churches and holy orders signed up to help implement this new model of education. Yes, it had some tragic consequences. But that does not establish genocide. However it does yield some take-aways about churches implementing government policy.

I ran into this same conundrum while working for the NGO World Vision in Mozambique. Americans prefer the term PVO or private voluntary organization. It describes who these entities are, not who they aren't. USAID calls them "carriers". This always made me uneasy. Government support meant the scale of resources, and therefore the volumes, were much higher. You could help more people. But you always felt the constraints and pressures of public policy. The PVO Mennonite Central Committee could export farmer-donated food-aid in sacks stamped simply "In the name of Christ". But the public policy of separation of church and state meant World Vision could not do so. The sacks were marked with USAID insignia. I am over-simplifying this a bit, in order to point out that church organizations implementing government-funded schools had little wiggle-room. They had to comply with government policy, because he who pays the fiddler calls the tune. I was not comfortable working in such an agency as a missionary, so I moved on.

As a result of this unholy alliance, good reputations are being tarnished. Revisionism is ripe when statues start to fall. I will mention only three samples, enough to make my point, but this is not at all a comprehensive list.

The first sample, and one of the best, is Egerton Ryerson. I mentioned earlier that the social innovation of Bishop Comenius of Czechia reached Upper Canada through Pennsylvania. Comenius died in 1670. Egerton Ryerson was born in 1803. During this 133-year gap, public education systems sprang up across Europe and then in the colonies too. It goes without saying education-for-all is now universally regarded as a virtue. Although education and "schooling" are not synonymous.

Ryerson became a Methodist minister, and an educator. He was devout, well-educated, unselfish and kind. He does not deserve what has happened to him. He is responsible more than anyone else for the advent of universally accessible, government funded public schools in Upper Canada, and consequently, one might say in English Canada. His Christian faith informed his life's work - creating public education. Until recently, he was much revered.

It is worth noting Ryerson counted many indigenous leaders among his friends and he was greatly admired by them, including the chief of the Mississauga Nation just outside where Toronto now is. Both Ryerson and the chiefs well understood the challenge indigenous youth faced in acquiring skills they would need to live in an increasingly agricultural and industrial society.

A college in downtown Toronto was later named after him - Ryerson Polytechnic Institute. It was later upgraded to Ryerson University. But his name was recently removed as a result of escalating revisionism. This all began a few years ago when students and indigenous activists began defacing Ryerson's statue at the university named after him. Not only was Ryerson's statue torn down, it was beheaded! Such was the rage. Of course, we did what Canadians do in a crisis; we formed a commission. The result was the removal of the statue and renaming the university. It is now Toronto Metropolitan University, hardly an inspiring name.

The complaint was that Ryerson was the "author" of the Canadian indigenous residential schools system. This is an overstatement. The annihilation of Ryerson's reputation rests upon a short report he wrote setting out his ideas for schools for aboriginal youth in southern Ontario. A man who was long considered to be one of the most progressive forces in pre-Confederation history is now considered part of a cultural genocide, or for some, just genocide.

In 1847, at the request of the then-Superintendent of Indigenous Affairs of the colonial government of Upper Canada, Ryerson wrote by hand a letter to the superintendent setting out his suggestions for the establishment of Industrial Schools for Aboriginal Youth. While he did not use the term "residential schools", he was of the view that the students should reside at the schools because their training was to include courses to equip them to become involved in farming, either as farm workers or as farm owners. These schools were planned for indigenous people in the enlarging farming areas of southern Ontario, and were designed for that purpose. In the 1830s through 1850, Upper Canada saw very large waves of immigration and increasing agricultural settlement throughout southern and central Ontario.

Read in the context of southern Ontario in 1847 and Ryerson's faith, it's a pretty good report. Ultimately, that report overshadowed all his achievements. He wrote, toward the end of the report: "It would be a gratifying result to see graduates of our Indian industrial schools become overseers of some the largest farms in Canada, nor will it be less gratifying to see them industrious and prosperous farmers on their own account."

The words quoted above clearly were not written in contemplation of genocide. That is clearly not their intent. Hitler would never have written such words about the Jews. In condemning our ancestors, we very often don't take the time to thoroughly know the facts and understand the context of their acts. Condemnation is so much easier, and sadly for some, satisfying.

I did not cry when the statue of Cecil Rhodes was pulled down in Capetown, but I did cry when the statue of Archbishop Desmond Tutu was torn down in Nelson Mandela Bay. One was Commerce, the other Christianity.

I did not cry when the statue of Edward Colston was pulled down in Bristol, but I did cry when the statue of Egerton Ryerson' was pulled down in Toronto. One was a slaver, the other was a man of integrity.

Another tragic incident is the resolve of the City of Toronto to change the name of its east-west thoroughfare, Dundas Street. When I went to school, I was taught the reason it meanders through the city unlike most streets on city-father Simcoe's square grid, is it was an old "Indian trail".

On 6 June 2020, a Black Lives Matter protest rally was staged on Dundas Street in downtown Toronto, Canada. The rally gave birth to a petition, soon bearing over 14,000 signatures, demanding the name of Dundas Street be changed. The petition claimed Dundas, a British politician, was responsible for many thousands of Africans being transported and delivered into slavery between 1793 and 1807, when the British parliament passed the Slave Trade Act. The organizers submitted their petition to Toronto City Hall and demanded action.

City Council asked its staff to prepare a report for Council's consideration, which they did. The report was short, about five paragraphs, according to journalists, and largely repeated the petitioners' allegations. Shortly thereafter, Council accepted the petitioners' demands and resolved to change the name of Dundas Street, although they did not agree upon a new name, nor have they done that to the time of writing this book.

But the movement to eliminate the name "Dundas" did not start in Toronto. Several years earlier a similar issue raged in Scotland, where Dundas was an historical icon. What began as an effort to affix a "contextual plaque" to a statue of Dundas morphed into a raging debate among historians and others as to what the plaque should say relative to the role of Dundas in the abolition efforts of his time. There is evidence this debate came to the attention of the BLM folks in Canada and likely played a large part in their crusade against Dundas and his namesake street.

The BLM petitioners can be commended for their organization skills and powers of persuasion. But their grasp of history and commitment to the truth is, at the least, debatable. A thorough analysis of the responsibility, if any, of Henry Dundas for the slave traffic in the 14 years following 1793 would easily consume a large book, or perhaps several. The following will suffice for our purposes.

Henry Dundas, a Scotsman, was born in 1742. He became a lawyer, and later arguably the most powerful politician in Britain in the late 18th century and early 19th century, second only to the legendary British Prime Minister, William Pitt, with whom Dundas served. In time, Dundas was created First Viscount Melville. He held three of the most senior cabinet positions during his career.

In 1792, William Wilberforce put forward a resolution (not a bill) in the British House of Commons, condemning the slave trade and calling for its abolition. Regrettably, it failed. Opposition to slavery met strong opposition, not only in the Commons, but in the House of Lords and even in the royal family, which at that time still had political influence.

Wilberforce tried again in 1793. Again, the motion was at risk of being defeated. Dundas stepped into the debate and moved an amendment to insert the word "gradually", signifying that abolition would take some time – from four to six years – to accomplish. The resolution, with the amendment, passed.

Of course, it was still just a resolution, not law. It required much work and political pressure to bring the matter to a vote on abolition in 1807, when parliament passed the <u>Slave Trade Act</u>. That Act abolished the trade, but not slavery, in the British empire. It was not until 1833, long after the death of Dundas in 1811, that parliament passed the <u>Slavery Abolition Act</u> to end slavery throughout the empire.

There are two well researched and argued positions among history scholars on Dundas and slavery.

The anti-Dundas folks say he delayed abolition by insisting in the 1793 resolution that it be a "gradual" process. They claim this directly caused about 600,000 Africans transported to North America between 1793 and 1807 to be unnecessarily delivered into slavery before the trade was abolished. This view – and no competing view – was the basis of the petition submitted to Toronto City Council and the very brief "report" submitted by its staff.

Defenders of Dundas take a very different view. They say Dundas sought a "gradual" process, because he feared a precipitous action would come without the vital support of British colonial legislatures in Jamaica and other Caribbean islands, which would be necessary to enforce abolition of the trade. He feared the trade would "go underground" and become impossible to extinguish. In fact, there is evidence that Dundas had made some progress with those colonial legislatures as early as 1793, but he needed more time. Opponents of Dundas conveniently overlook the fact that Wilberforce's resolution was just that – an expression of the opinion of the House, and not the legal instrument of abolition of the slave trade. It recognized there was work to be done to make abolition a reality. Defenders say Dundas facilitated abolition of the slave trade by the shrewd deployment of his political acumen and power. He understood politics as the art of the possible.

These competing views of Dundas and slavery are irreconcilable.

There are other facts about Dundas, which should give, at the least, pause before condemning him as a supporter of the slave trade. He began his working life as a lawyer in Scotland. There he gained notoriety for defending Joseph Knight, a black man, who was seized and enslaved in Jamaica and transported to Scotland, where he attempted to escape from his master, for which he was charged with a criminal offense. Dundas famously prevailed and won an acquittal. Dundas' argument in court survives today. Among other things, he said, "As Christianity gained ground in different nations, slavery was abolished ... (I hope) for the honour of <u>Scotland</u>, that the <u>Supreme Court</u> of this country would not be the only court that would give its sanction to so barbarous a claim ... Human nature, my Lords, spurns at the thought of slavery among any part of our species." Hardly the words of a coddler of slave traders.

The mayor of Toronto, John Tory, in voting for name change of Dundas Street, said disdainfully of Henry Dundas, "He never set foot in this country", as though that was remotely relevant to the debate. But Tory was correct. Dundas never travelled to England's North American colonies. But his footprint was left there. It was Henry Dundas, as Secretary of the Home Office, who in 1791 appointed John Graves Simcoe as the first Lieutenant Governor of Upper Canada in 1791. Simcoe was a British Army general and noted abolitionist. Immediately upon arrival in the colony, Simcoe convened the elected Legislative Assembly and told them: "The principles of the <u>British Constitution</u> do not admit of that slavery which <u>Christianity condemns</u>. The moment I assume the Government of Upper Canada under no modification will I assent to a law that discriminates by dishonest policy between natives of Africa, America, or Europe."

Simcoe's ardent opposition to slavery, the slave trade and discrimination was well-known, including to Dundas. While he failed to abolish slavery in Upper Canada, his interventions did have the effect of turning public opinion, over time, against it, so it became less prevalent. Eventually, it was abolished in the whole empire after Simcoe's term. The idea that a supporter of the slave trade would appoint Simcoe is not supportable.

As Home Secretary, Dundas implemented other progressive policies supporting the rights of black people, and indigenous peoples as well as the conquered Quebecois. He refused demands to create British Army regiments comprised of black slaves. He understood very well the value of Britain's defensive alliance with indigenous peoples in the years before the War of 1812. He gave written instructions to the British Governor in Quebec to treat indigenous peoples with respect "...securing to them the peaceable and quiet possession of the Lands which they have hitherto occupied as their hunting Grounds, and such others as may enable them to procure a comfortable subsistence for themselves and their families." He required all colonial legislation in Lower Canada (Quebec) be translated into French – perhaps the first bilingualism law in what ultimately became Canada.

Changing the name of a street – even a street known by one name for over 200 years - is not, in the overall scheme of things, of immense importance, even though the costs of doing so are estimated to range from $6 million to $10 million. And that does not include costs merchants and businesses along the route will suffer in adapting their printed materials to the change. The inconvenience to adjacent municipalities, like the City of Mississauga – named for the indigenous tribe of that name – who share Dundas Street, but see no reason to change its name, will pass in time. And of course, settling on a new name is likely to be a divisive exercise.

But this business of changing the name of Dundas Street, however trivial in itself, gives us a vivid example of how easily well-meaning people, and their eager-to-oblige governments, can be seriously mislead by those who are content to trash, not only the reputation of an honorable person, but any respect for Truth in presenting their argument. In this case, Toronto City Council relied upon a petition and a five-paragraph report prepared by wholly unqualified City staff and riddled with inaccuracies. There are no winners in this affair – not even those who pushed the name change.

Dundas was not a saint. Who among us is? But he was not, even remotely, the monster portrayed by his detractors. Perhaps the last word on Henry Dundas should go to William Wilberforce, the champion of abolition and Dundas' contemporary, who more than anyone would have cause to detest one who fit the description of him by Toronto City Staff. After the <u>Abolition Act, 1807</u> passed, Wilberforce wrote, "About a year before he (Dundas) died ... we saw one another, and at first, I thought he was passing on, but he stopped and called out, 'Ah Wilberforce, how do you do?' And gave me a hearty shake by the hand. I would have given a thousand pounds for that shake. I never saw him afterwards."

I would think $6 million would be better spent securing clean drinking water on one of the many indigenous reserves that have been waiting for that since PM Justin Trudeau promised it in 2016. We don't know yet what name will replace Dundas, but I would guess that only missionaries will be able to pronounce it. There is a time for revisionism. For example, I am convinced Eswatini is a better name for that country than Swaziland. I am less convinced that Azania is a better name for South Africa. Or that New Zealand should be renamed Aotearoa. However, I think that renaming Dundas Street is just *ad hominem*.

Could there be such a thing as "reputational genocide"? If there is cultural genocide, then why not reputational genocide too? We build monuments to remind us of where we came from. We name streets, highways and universities to esteem those who have made great contributions to our society. (Like Indiana and Indianapolis, which esteem indigenous people.) Without these reminders, we can lose our way. According to the UN definition of "genocide", here is the logic behind my question: "intent to destroy → a religious group → causing serious bodily or **mental harm** to members of the group". George Washington owned slaves, so should the capital of the USA be re-named? Is it legitimate for an inclusive society to selectively exclude historical figures?

Finally, we need to look at what is currently happening to Professor Frances Widdowson, a Canadian scholar. She was fired from a tenured position at Mount Royal University for the sin of suggesting residential schools, while harmful, did have some educational value for some students. Given an opportunity to recant, she wouldn't. It reminds me of Martin Luther facing charges of heresy at the Diet of Worms. "Here I stand. I can do no other."

Her response was to ask her employer a question: "Is MRU an academic or an activist institution?" Do academics no longer value discourse? Are they not seeking the truth? Her dismissal was a violation of civil liberties. She stated her considered opinion. Freedom of expression was not permitted, not even freedom of thought. Diversity of opinion was flushed down the drain. In a world of propaganda, Truth is a conspiracy theory.

Then she was invited by a faculty member to speak at the University of Lethbridge. A student revolt, which involved many faculty, ensued. But the University said they would permit her to speak as required by the University's commitment to freedom of speech. That lasted about a day, and then she was barred from speaking.

Frances Widdowson and her husband have been a target of academia since at least 2009 when they co-wrote a book entitled <u>Disrobing the Aboriginal Industry</u>. Since she wrote this book, there has been billions of dollars poured into the indigenous file, by all levels of government. Some has come in settlement of lawsuits, and some as policy or in implementing TRC "Calls to Action". Yet many indigenous communities still struggle and have no clean drinking water. I can't imagine where all the money wound up. And the taps are still on full. It's a tragedy, not just for Canada, but for the indigenous people. Money doesn't seem to begin to solve the issues.

In closing, let me pause to remind the reader about the apocryphal story of the Almo massacre of two hundred and ninety five whites by Shoshone-Bannock in 1861 in Idaho. According to Thomas King's research, it never happened. It was fiction. As he writes on page 8: "A right proper Western". Implied of course is that attacks on white settlers were being exaggerated as propaganda to validate white aggression. I accept the finding of his research – that this incident was apocryphal.

It does not take long before revisionism turns into propaganda. Before misinformation leads to book-burning. Before bent attitudes lead to violence. Before intolerance leads to a twilight zone of polarization. Conserving is very,

very important. It is what the indigenous peoples of North America want, after all - to conserve their ways of life. Conservation is a virtue. So – to be fair - why is leading us, turning into misleading us?

11. EPILOGUE

God help us to find innovative and definitive solutions with open minds and mutual respect. As for me, I still believe in the missionary vocation. It has made a huge social contribution, and its work is unfinished.

"Last words" have a special place in our perception of who the speaker was and why they mattered to us. Matthew and Mark recorded the last words Jesus spoke while he walked among us. They were, and remain, the inspiration and the aim of Christian mission work. They tell us not only what missionaries do, but why they do it, now and in the past. Matthew's record tells us that, of all Jesus spoke on earth, he reserved the words below for his last. So, I can do no better than end this book with Jesus' words...

"All authority in heaven and on earth has been given to me.

Therefore go and make disciples of all nations,

baptizing them in the name of the Father and of the Son and of the Holy Spirit, and teaching them to obey everything I have commanded you.

And surely I am with you always, to the very end of the age."